T0313160

Emerging Technologies in Healthcare

Emerging Technologies in Healthcare

Suzanne Moss Richins

CRC Press
Taylor & Francis Group
Boca Raton London New York

CRC Press is an imprint of the
Taylor & Francis Group, an **informa** business
A PRODUCTIVITY PRESS BOOK

CRC Press
Taylor & Francis Group
6000 Broken Sound Parkway NW, Suite 300
Boca Raton, FL 33487-2742

First issued in hardback 2019

© 2015 by Taylor & Francis Group, LLC
CRC Press is an imprint of Taylor & Francis Group, an Informa business

No claim to original U.S. Government works

ISBN-13: 978-1-4822-6262-9 (hbk)

Visit the Taylor & Francis Web site at
http://www.taylorandfrancis.com

and the CRC Press Web site at
http://www.crcpress.com

Contents

Preface

Most people associate innovation with healthcare. During the last century, scientists discovered miracle drugs, genome sequencing, minimally invasive surgery, transplants, stem cells, the ability to grow new tissue and organs, and more recently, both 3D and 4D printing of tissue and organs. The enactment of the Patient Protection and Affordable Care Act (Obamacare) has triggered the need for more innovation due to the focus on the health of the population with global payments to accountable care organizations.

Urgent care clinics and retail clinics have moved patient care away from the emergency room to less costly and more convenient delivery of care. Telemedicine makes it even more convenient since the patient can access care anytime, from anywhere, 24 hours a day. It also creates more access to limited specialists without the need for travel.

The implementation of electronic medical records (EMRs) provides two advantages. First, the EMR ensures that the patient's history is readily available to each and every care provider, which creates a more coordinated effort in patient care and decreases the possibility of competing therapies and drug–drug interactions, along with avoiding the duplication of tests. Second, the collection of patient data through the EMR also provides a rich database for studying disease and therapeutics.

The wars in Afghanistan and Iraq focused attention on the need for better prosthetics and the use of robotics to restore function to these injured veterans. These innovations, focused on the veterans, also help trauma victims and those born with congenital anomalies since the intent is to create optimal function and independence for the patient.

Advancement in healthcare delivery systems creates an ecosystem beginning with diagnosis, treatment, and ensuring optimal health status. New discoveries include prescription drug classification in new categories such as kinase drugs that inhibit the growth of enzymes in cancer. Personalized medicine utilizes designer drugs specific to the DNA of the patient and the disease. Designer drugs use the DNA of the disease (like cancer) or the DNA of an infection and match it with the DNA of the patient to target the specific cells in need of treatment intervention.

Scientists have discovered new ways to activate the patient's natural defense and immunity system by stimulating the thymus gland. With the advent of Obamacare's focus on population health, individuals need to take charge of their own health. New apps for smartphones, such as the iPhone HealthKit allow individuals to monitor their own vital signs, progress, and goal tracking. A way to foster the natural alignment of the body through exercise can eliminate stress on joints that creates osteoarthritis.

New apps and sensors that transmit data allow seniors to age in place and remain independent, creating a better quality of life, which is less of an expense than institutionalizing the elderly. Technological advancements can also remind seniors to take their medication and stimulate activity.

About the Author

Suzanne Moss Richins, DHA, is known as an early adopter of technology and innovation. As a senior leader in healthcare, she was one of the first to look at using analytics to structure staffing schedules—based on patient arrival acuity to the emergency department for her master's thesis. The methodology was adopted throughout Intermountain Healthcare (Salt Lake City, Utah) and various other well-known healthcare systems. While serving on the American Hospital Association board and the Joint Commission Advisory Committee, Dr. Richins conducted her dissertation on patient satisfaction prior to the adoption of these standards by both of these respected organizations. Her latest work is in using analytics to predict patient outcomes and improve quality. She also teaches DBA, DHA, and DNP students for various universities.

Dr. Richins earned her nursing degree from Weber State University (Ogden, Utah), her professional arts degree from St. Joseph's College (North Wyndam, Maine), her MBA from Utah State University (Logan), and her doctorate in healthcare administration at the Medical University of South Carolina (Charleston). She earned her degrees while advancing from staff nurse to manager of the operating rooms, director of emergency and urgent care clinics, director of medical/surgical services, administrator of freestanding surgical centers, and chief operating officer.

Due to her varied education and experience, Dr. Richins currently provides consultation and advice to clients about software for electronic medical records, revenue cycle management, and predictive and retrospective analytics. She is the senior vice president for healthcare at Global Targeting, Inc.

Chapter 1

Telehealth, Telemedicine, and eHealth

Two phenomena came together during the implementation of the Patient Protection and Affordable Care Act: a predicted shortage of physicians and advances in technology. Use of technology could potentially solve the physician shortage. In addition, the baby boomer generation continues to age and require more healthcare. Technology may allow them to age in place at home while receiving monitored healthcare services.

Several terms describe how patients receive care through technology. They include *telemedicine, telehealth, telecare,* and *eVisits,* and, often, the terms are used interchangeably even though they have different meanings. The Health Resources and Services Administration (HRSA) defines telehealth as a function that uses telecommunication (videoconferencing, imaging, streaming media, and wireless communication) to provide clinical healthcare over a distance. It may include education, support, or healthcare administration.

Telehealth means the use of audio-visual technology to connect with a patient. It is not limited by the discipline using the technology.

Telemedicine means the use of audio-visual technology by a physician or other provider in a remote location to interact and consult with patients or other practitioners.

Telecare means the monitoring of patients' vital signs, activity, and physiological signs and providing an alert or intervention based on changes in any of these three categories.

eVisits encompass any patient and healthcare personnel via audio-visual technology.

The Centers for Medicare and Medicaid Services (CMS) announced on July 3, 2014, that they added payments for telehealth visits. Qualifying visits include annual wellness visits and psychotherapy. CMS deemed telehealth visits to be similar to professional consults conducted in an office setting (Health and Human Services 2014a), which qualify them for reimbursement. At the end of the comment period (September 12, 2014), 400 manufacturers and providers supported the expansion of telehealth services.

Telehealth

In 2012, the Veterans Administration (VA) reached 500,000 veterans using 1.4 million telehealth visits. In 2013, this increased to over 600,000 telehealth visits at 151 VA medical centers and 705 community-based outpatient clinics with 1.7 million episodes of care or a 22% increase in the use of this technology. Bed days were also reduced by 59% and admissions were reduced by 35%. Patients who used telehealth visits saved $2,000 each in their reduced out-of-pocket expenses (Bowman 2014).

UCLA physicians provide telehealth visits through a product called *LiveHealth Online*. Anthem Blue Cross covers this benefit at $49 a copay for this visit. The service focuses on nonemergency conditions such as coughs, rashes, and sore throats (Gorman 2014) (Figure 1.1).

As a growing delivery model, 20 states and the District of Columbia added the requirement that commercial payors add

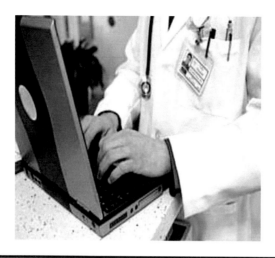

Figure 1.1 A virtual physician visit. (From Gorman, A., *Kaiser Health News*, September 16, 2014, http://capsules.kaiserhealthnews.org.)

telehealth to the coverage they provide for Medicaid; however, Medicaid has no provision for home health agencies to use this technology (Wicklund 2014a).

Homeless and displaced veterans often receive no healthcare. Recovering addicts and the homeless veterans at the Talbert House can access telehealth 24 hours a day free of charge. Anthem Blue Cross and Blue Shield donated this service. These individuals often cannot access traditional healthcare because they usually work at low-paying jobs where the hours are inflexible; they lack insurance and often have no access to transportation. This service addresses all of these issues (Bernard-Kuhn 2014) (Figure 1.2).

Forbes predicts that telehealth revenues will reach $2 billion by 2018. The trend continues to grow and busy individuals like the convenience of accessing care wherever they might be. In 2014, 42% of hospitals used telehealth. Some employers offer this benefit to avoid costly emergency room visits. "Online Care Group, which uses American Well's platform for its service, has about 500,000 consultants. On-staff physicians fulfill more than 90% of consultations... Staff doctors communicate

Figure 1.2   Doctors on Demand with virtual visits. Doctors on Demand has an iOS and Android app for tablets and smartphones, as well as Kindle and desktop Web versions. (Screenshot from Doctors on Demand. From Somerville, H., *San Jose Mercury News,* **August 8, 2014, http://www.mercurynews.com.)**

with each other via Microsoft Lync and use Citrix GoToMeeting for webinars and training sessions" (Diana 2014, p. 1).

The growth in technology allows for the use of wireless products to provide virtual care. Individual adoption of technology and its ubiquitous use makes it possible to connect patients at a low cost using their own technology (Figure 1.3).

Mississippi leads the country in terms of using telehealth. People who live in rural Appalachia often cannot obtain the medical care they need. To solve this problem, the University of Mississippi Medical Center (UMMC) started its first telehealth program in 2013, known as *telemergency*; and since then, it has expanded to several hospitals, clinics, and physicians. Unfortunately, the regulations and laws do not match the capabilities and patient needs. Therefore, Senator Lott is sponsoring a bill to allow physicians licensed in one state to care for patients in another state using this technology (Pender 2014).

As insurers tackle the problem of ensuring a healthy population given the change from volume to value, they increasingly

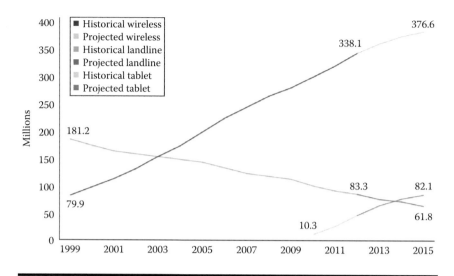

Figure 1.3   The growth of wireless products. Healthcare providers use common technology combined with software to complete this transaction. (Data from IBIS*World* Industry Reports, 2014, www.ibisworld.com.)

look for technology that will aid them in keeping people healthy. Monitoring patients at home makes achievement of this goal possible. Success stories include one from Vidant Health where they targeted discharged patients suffering from pulmonary and cardiac problems. These patients were asked to complete the Patient Activation Measurement (PAM) survey. Depending upon the score, they were enrolled in the program, which starts with a visit by a telehealth nurse technician (TNT). A normal home care assessment was conducted for safety along with a review of the discharge medication list. Subsequently, remote monitoring and medication compliance occurred. The result was a 67% reduction in hospitalizations and a 68% reduction in hospital bed days (Wicklund 2014a).

Since home care nurses spend a lot of their time driving between patients, prioritizing patient needs can increase efficiency. Remote monitoring allows them to prioritize care. Patients are often poor historians and do not always share accurate data. Improvement occurs through the use of a remote monitoring system that provides real and accurate values. Some patients only need a phone call while others require an assessment.

Remote monitoring combined with electronic records accessible through a cloud ensures coordination between disciplines. The physical therapist may change the order of patient visits based on the home care nurse assessment, administration of drugs, or therapies. Real-time alerts can help them maximize their time to improve productivity and efficiency.

Bright Insight reports that more than 3 million people worldwide live at home while engaging in remote monitoring by a professional. The report noted that this represents $5.8 billion in 2013. The largest segment of monitoring involves cardiac monitoring to mitigate the effects of dysrhythmia with timely interventions (Baum 2014a).

In a similar program, Care at Hand also provides a survey to patients prior to discharge. The survey contains 15 questions linked to an algorithm that identifies problems and predicts issues for both nonmedical and medical problems. Of the questions, 60% focus on organic, medical problems involving diabetes, lung diseases, and heart problems. The nurse's aide provides an update at each visit by asking these same questions and transmitting the answers. An alert goes to the supervisor to provide an opportunity for intervention before a problem occurs. This program demonstrated a 40% decrease in readmissions post-discharge (Schwartz 2014a).

A Medicaid experiment in New York focused on the most expensive patients to see what could be done to improve their compliance with their personal treatment plans. Sixty-seven patients and their 15 care managers were enrolled in a pilot program that used a mobile application. The result of this intensive monitoring through data capture and patient self-reporting was a 12% increase in medication adherence and a 7% increase in compliance to the treatment plan (Wicklund 2014b).

Twelve million people suffer from sleep apnea. The treatment consists of continuous pressurized air pressure, which pushes oxygen into the lungs to prevent apnea. Like most interventions, people do not always comply with the treatment plan. With machine-to-machine (M2M) data delivery, alerts are sent to the company that provides the equipment (usually a home care agency) and to the individual. If the individual misses a night of use, the messaging starts. M2M alerts eliminated manual phone calls to patients. The software also sends other patient engagement messages like congratulations on their compliance and improvement usage. The software reduced labor by 59%, improving adherence to 70% of the treatment plan every 30 days (Leventhal 2014).

American Well provides an app that a physician uses to record visits with a patient. Then, the patient and/or family member can review the recorded visit later. Often, patients cannot remember everything that the physician said or they may want to review it again. Also, family members responsible for the patient may want an update. The American Well app provides this convenience (American Well 2014).

Another good use of telehealth materialized in a study of children at UC Davis Children's Hospital; hospital staff were able to teleconference with friends and family, which improved the quality of life during the children's hospital stay. A total of 232 children took part in the study. Their stress level was checked on admission and discharge using the Parent Guardian Stress Survey. Their scores were compared with 133 children who did not use the teleconference capability. Those who did use it had a greater reduction in stress levels (Yang et al. 2014).

The growth in the telehealth industry was identified as a new trend by some nonhealthcare businesses. For instance, Verizon created a new platform designed for use in this medium. They recognize both the convenience and the expedience that transpires through telehealth. For this reason, Verizon developed Verizon Virtual Visits, which competes with Teladoc, MDLive, and American Well. Payors, providers, and self-insured businesses are all looking for new methods to connect physicians and patients. Users connect through an app or patient portal to initiate the virtual visit (Wicklund 2014c).

Telemedicine

The Centers for Medicaid and Medicare Services regulate the types of telemedicine they approve and reimburse. They define telemedicine as a real-time two-way communication between a patient and a physician. They use interactive video and audio communication during this visit. Currently, the visit can only take place between a patient and physician who is licensed in the same state as the patient (CMS 2014).

The Federation of State Medical Boards adopted a policy that requires videoconferencing (2014a). The policy states that audio is not enough to create a physician–patient relationship. Videoconferencing can be used through Skype, FaceTime, or through the use of the Microsoft Kinect game controller. Kinect allows healthcare personnel to easily connect with patients at home for an examination, a physical therapy visit using the gaming features, or a myriad of other telemedicine reasons such as mentoring other physicians in remote locations. Telemedicine allows other providers to enter the sterile field without contaminating it (Bailey and Jensen 2013).

Insurers embrace telemedicine and telehealth at different levels. For instance, UnitedHealth reports a portion of its $7 billion primary care service occurs through these new modalities and categories; $30 billion of its $100 billion in medical services to performance-based reimbursement. Their outreach in telemedicine occurred through 350,000 contacts and 4,500 daily home visits per day. In addition, it remotely monitors 20,000 people, most of which have cardiovascular disease (Morrissey 2014).

Maricopa Integrated Health Systems in Phoenix, Arizona reports that it saved $74,000 in its first year of operation by offering telemedicine to its employees. They reported that convenience was a factor for the employees who would normally access care through an urgent care clinic. Leaders of the health system expect more savings as technology continues to improve (Jayanthi 2014a).

Not every hospital can afford specialists; therefore, telemedicine provides this expertise through remote monitoring. One example is a software system that monitors and identifies patient parameters for any two of the risks, which include elevated lactic acid levels, systemic inflammatory response, an order for blood cultures, and hypotension to determine if a patient is developing sepsis. An epidemiologist offsite monitors these values and contacts the physician advising that the patient needs a consult (Wild 2014).

A study of 1,257 preemie babies from 12 different centers showed that telemedicine review of the eye identified the service needed for those with retinal changes. Nonphysicians were trained to read images that were sent to them, which were previously reviewed by ophthalmologists. When compared with the physician readings, the nonphysician readers were 98% accurate. These outcomes show that telemedicine can provide an accurate service for multiple centers at once, which increases efficiency by using specialty care wisely (Goth 2014a).

Aging in place is one term for allowing seniors to remain at home in familiar surroundings in the best possible health status for the individual. There are several different ways to monitor people unobtrusively and to help them stay safe in their own homes. Assisted living centers and long-term care centers use radar systems to monitor patient movement. The radar is connected to a system that sends an alert to the person caring for the patient. One of them relies on urban radar, a product used by the military to monitor people in buildings. The radar can identify when a person falls on the floor and can activate an alert so someone can respond and assist the individual. Radar works by bouncing waves against objects and then creating an image based on these waves (Wang 2014).

Readmission to the hospital within 30 days of discharge often occurs due to noncompliance with the treatment plan, which includes not taking medications properly or skipping doses altogether. To solve this problem, Porteus Digital Health developed a system that contains a patch worn on the body and an ingestible sensor that tracks medicine usage. The technology can be embedded right into the medication pill, which transmits the data to the patch and relays it to a smart app. The absence of expected data triggers an alert to someone who can check on the patient using Porteus (2014).

Another product relies on sensors. As hospitals take on the role of population health, the role extends from hospitalization to monitoring health status in the home. The home-based monitoring system collects biometric data from the patient and from medical devices at the home and enters it into the electronic record. If a patient falls or other parameters change for the worse, the sensors identify the fall or change and send an alert that initiates a response. The idea behind home monitoring is to reduce the $31 million spent on preventable hospitalizations (Wicklund 2014c).

A chair containing the first contact-free sensor approved by the Food and Drug Administration (FDA) monitors heart rate, respiration, and activity through movement allowing for monitoring to ensure that patients are upright and moving their upper body. This monitoring is especially important right after surgery to prevent post-op complications (Goth 2014b).

Telemedicine uses the data from mobile devices in conjunction with the signs and symptoms described by the patient for use as a differential diagnostic tool. In addition to the benefit of closely monitoring chronic conditions to keep them within normal limits, patient engagement ensures that the patient learns to understand his or her own condition and how to make changes in habits and choices that will lead toward a more healthy lifestyle. The Veterans Administration study found that the cost of caring for patients at home is 1.6% ($1,600/year versus $100,000) of what it costs to institutionalize a patient

(Eustis 2013). The Veterans Administration currently provides video consults at 800 sites involving 45 specialities, one of which is therapy for post-traumatic stress disorder (Landro 2014).

Based on these savings, it is no wonder that the high-growth projections for the telemedicine-dedicated device and software markets at $843 million in 2012 are anticipated to reach $2.9 billion by 2019. mHealth markets related to telemedicine were calculated at $1.4 billion and are anticipated to reach $1.5 trillion by 2019 due to the use of 7 billion smartphones with half that many connected to tablet devices all over the world (Eustis 2013).

Deloitte predicts that eVisits will total 100 million by the end of 2014. The use of eVisits will save $50–$60 billion for the year, which demonstrates a 400% growth rate since 2012. The routine urgent care visits fit the eVisit model while more complex problems will require an in-person visit (Hall 2014).

Instead of admitting patients for inpatient rehabilitation, physicians and physical therapists can use the gaming technology in Kinect to provide therapy. Since patients in the hospital setting often acquire hospital-related infections (Su 2013), the gaming technology encourages patients to perform their exercises at home to avoid the hospital exposure while playing a game. The ease of exercising in the home and using the game makes the exercise more interesting and accessible and does not expose patients to germs found in healthcare facilities.

Children in rehab often respond to robots and games when they do not respond to people. Since rehab often involves repetition of movements to exercise affected body parts, the children find it boring and often refuse to continue. Through the use of robots and games, researchers at Georgia Tech were able to engage these pediatric patients to increase their repetitive exercise. They use humanoid robots and ask the children to teach them how to play a game of Angry Birds. When interacting with the robot, children increased their therapy by 40% compared to 7% when interacting with a human adult (Reader 2014).

The use of robots to provide therapy and as an intervention method continues to advance with new and interesting capacities. For instance, a bio-bot made of hydrogel works like normal muscle with less limitation on motion than current prostheses. The Meka robotic arm uses artificial intelligence to anticipate the next movement and can improvise music when used to drum as an accompaniment to other musicians. A haptic training robot teaches medical students how to conduct physical exams. The haptic robot teaches the student how the body actually feels. It moves the hand on these human-like body parts so the student learns the proper way to conduct the exam and he or she will understand what normal and abnormal feels like. Kernerworks' TraumaSim™ screams and bleeds to simulate a trauma victim's responses to losing a limb. It responds to treatment and breathes just like a human victim. Surgical robots can bore into the brain to eat a tumor and another one can crawl down the throat into the stomach to eat the tumor there. Veebot uses imaging to find the vein, draws blood, and then labels the specimen for processing (Wagner 2014).

Mississippi ranks second in terms of the highest population affected by diabetes. With a total expenditure of $2.7 billion annually, the cost of care for diabetes totals nearly 3% of the state's economy (gross state product). For this reason, the governor signed a bill for case management of low-income patients diagnosed with diabetes. The bill also includes a measure that requires the private insurance companies to provide care to the state's Medicaid and state employee health plans with reimbursement for medical providers who provide services via computer screens and telecommunications, at the same reimbursement rate as that paid for an in-person medical visit (Vestal 2014). This foray into intensive case management using telemedicine signifies a change in addressing the costs and health of the population. The idea is to closely monitor these patients, prevent complications, increase compliance to treatment, increase quality of life, and ultimately reduce large expenditures.

Another approach focuses on identification of pre-diabetic patients, which allows for prevention. Patients receive instruction and an app for physical fitness through eWellness. Over a 6-month period, patients receive instructions for increasingly difficult exercises that last approximately 45 minutes. A physical therapist monitors them remotely to ensure the exercises are done correctly and at the same time provides encouragement and motivation to the patient to help them stay with the program. Insurers pay $3,000 per enrolled patient, which costs a lot less than allowing them to progress to become a diabetic patient (Baum 2014b).

Patients potentially suffering from a stroke only have 3 hours between onset of the clot and the optimal therapeutics from administering tPa, which dissolves the clot and diminishes the long-term effects of the stroke. Often, the decision to call 911 and the actual transport after the call exceeds this time limit. For this reason, the University of Virginia Health System instituted a project to shorten this time. The program uses a telemedicine system to connect the patient with a neurologist and paramedics through a program called *iTREAT* (Improving Treatment Times for Evaluation of Acute stroke via mobile Telemedicine) that uses a secure video link. This connection allows commencement of diagnostic protocols during patient transport (Page 2014).

Another study by the Center for Technology and Aging (Desjardin 2014) predicts that over the next 25 years, the U.S. healthcare system could save $200 billion. This savings projection can be realized by using a variety of technology applications and patient monitoring which will occur remotely. Most patients follow a daily routine with their eating, sleeping, physical activity, and elimination habits. eNeighbor tracks when and how participants spend their time. The system includes 11 sensors installed throughout patients' homes. Motion sensors hang on beds, walls, and refrigerators, toilets track all activity and note patterns. This early alert provides an opportunity for early intervention that prevents the need for costly services. In addition, Healthsense Care Alliance researchers noted that the rate of residents moving in and out of senior living facilities was reduced by 27% when remote monitoring was used (Desjardin 2014). Other sensors can provide alerts to changes in vital signs.

The benefits of telehealth revolve around the ability to provide complex and efficient care. Telehealth adoption rates vary widely across the nation mostly attributed to the differences in state policies. Alaska provides the most telehealth services at 75%. Arkansas, South Dakota, and Maine hover around a 70% adoption rate (McCann 2014a). The American Telemedicine Association reports that more than 50% of U.S. hospitals use telehealth to deliver care to their patients. They state that 200 telemedicine networks served more than 3,500 facilities in 2014 (Landro 2014).

Patients call in for their appointment at a prescribed time. Some virtual visits include a waiting room with patient education materials specific to the patient's concern or diagnosis (Comstock 2013). In the virtual waiting room, patients are not exposed to infectious diseases carried by other patients in a physical waiting room.

Through the use of Skype or FaceTime, a patient can meet face-to-face with a provider with many of the same benefits of an in-person encounter. Telephone-only visits do not provide the opportunity to view patients for nonverbal clues about their condition or to examine them. With telehealth, the provider can look to see if swelling is evident in the ankles, examine lesions, and facial expressions. Research shows that both patients (94%) and providers prefer telehealth. Of physicians, 60% also prefer to add data from a mobile device to provide a more complete picture of the patient that includes signs of distress, facial expressions, and fatigue (GeeksWorld 2014).

For geriatric patients and their families, these telehealth opportunities save them the frustration of finding transportation and time waiting in a doctor's office. Family members often need to take half-a-day away from work in order to take a family member to these appointments.

Blue Cross and Blue Shield (BCBS) of Minnesota noted that since 2010, their coverage for telemedicine grew 200% per year. People pay $45 for the visit, which is 100% covered by BCBS. Most of the physicians in their network use Teledoc, which contains high-definition video. Teledoc reports that the list of conditions treated via telemedicine includes sinus problems, allergies, urinary tract infections, ear infections, and coughs (Mace 2014a).

The rise of urgent care clinics, also known as after-hours clinics, came about due to the demand by working adults who wanted an appointment outside of the normal 8:00 to 5:00 time frame provided by a traditional physician's office; however, these clinics were only open limited hours (usually until 9:00 P.M.). The retail clinics followed the same model; however, they also opened on weekends. With the advent of telemedicine, patients can access a physician 24/7 through the use of the technology.

Telehealth makes it possible to access specialty trained physicians from anywhere, even on the athletic field. About 60% of high schools have no athletic trainer available to evaluate potential concussion injuries incurred while playing sports. To ensure student safety and to identify a concussion early, northern Arizona schools utilize a robot equipped with a camera that transmits vital information to a neurologist to assess the athlete right on the sidelines of the sport (Monegain 2013).

In addition to the concussion service, Mayo Clinic offers the robot technology for athletics along with another program called *telestroke*. Other researchers identified the fact that 40% of Arizona residents live where there is no specialist for stroke care. These same specialists are available for these rural residents. When they arrive in a local emergency room, the ER physician can access the stroke specialist through telestroke (Monegain 2013).

Medtronic possesses a device that measures the velocity of hits to the head. The device, Reebok's CheckLight, is a soft cap that fits on the head underneath the player's helmet. It contains sensors that measure accelerations to the head. When dangerous acceleration occurs, a light turns on to alert the trainers and coach that the athlete needs attention (Mace 2014a).

University of Pennsylvania's Perelman School of Medicine physicians studied stroke response across the country. They identified the east and southeastern states as the stroke belt. Michael Mullen, M.D., noted that differences in identifying and treating stroke victims occur both within states, from county to county, and often within a county. Once the research team identifies these disparities, they provide the necessary intervention to both increase and treat stroke victims optimally by addressing the density of the population, the demographics, and the available resources for healthcare (Penn Medicine 2014).

Another researcher at Perelman, Claude Nguyen, M.D., developed an app for use in triaging stroke patients effectively. The app allows physicians to simultaneously perform multiple tasks needed to diagnose, treat, and enroll patients in clinical trial research. The app keeps track of the critical events such as when the symptoms first occurred, when the patient arrived at the hospital, the time images were taken, and when rt-PA was administered. All of this information creates an environment that optimizes the treatment course for a better stroke outcome (Penn Medicine 2014).

Another University of Pennsylvania alumni developed Flatiron Health, a program to connect doctors and cancer centers to one another in order to share data that is useful in making treatment decisions. They use de-identified data from patient charts in 200 cancer centers containing 550,000 cancer cases. The information is collected in OncoAnalytics where various treatments for specific cancers can be analyzed (Hay 2014).

On-the-job injuries in rural areas pose a greater threat to the employee due to response times and delays in treatment along with a lack of needed specialists. Telemedicine provides that link with specialists and injured employees. The technology uses equipment similar to an iPad that connects the physician and the patient. This technique is also used for industry compensation exams. It saves the employee and the employer travel costs and time while providing exactly the care needed. The state of Nevada uses this technology as part of their Workers' Compensation Program (Goldberg 2014).

Large employers contract with WellPoint, Teledoc, and other online services. These employers find that providing this access can increase productivity. An employee can use a computer in a private room for a physician or other practitioner visit. They can get their problem addressed and be back to work in the same amount of time as a break or a lunch hour. Benefits providers state that 18% of companies now offer this service. These visits typically cost $49 compared to $150 for an office visit (Coombs 2014).

Other rural health providers often provide services to a wide geographic area. For instance, most of Texas fits the rural health description with small populations scattered around the state. This definition makes it impossible to locate specialists proximal to the patient needs. Instead, patients rely on telemedicine for contact with specialists like psychiatrists. Instead of traveling 100 miles and waiting 3 to 6 months for an appointment, patients can make a telemedicine appointment and meet with a physician within 2 weeks. Even though Midland, Texas has one of the lowest unemployment rates, the stress and pressure of working in the oil fields takes its toll on patients through suicide, alcoholism, and other mental health problems (Gleason 2014). The ability to obtain needed healthcare in a timely manner provides the needed counsel and treatment prescribed by a physician.

Rural health includes American Indian reservations where there are few primary care physicians and no specialists. For instance, the Goshute Indians live on 113,000 acres in rural Utah. They now have access to both primary care and specialists through a program that originated in Utah.

The tribal leaders were able to access a grant to first bring Internet capabilities to the reservation. Then, a second grant connected them to TruClinic based in Salt Lake City, Utah. TruClinic utilizes Bluetooth technology to connect stethoscopes, glucose monitors, and blood pressure monitors to their mHealth solution (Wicklund 2013a).

Children in inner city schools often have no access to healthcare. Many are illegal immigrants and their parents are afraid they will be deported if they seek healthcare. Other minority parents work more than one job and have no benefits. They cannot take time off work to take a child to a provider for care. Hence, many inner city schools made cooperative agreements with universities that provide healthcare for these underserved children. In addition to normal care, they now use telehealth to access physicians in real time for consults (Wicklund 2013a).

The University of Pittsburg Medical Center Health System calls this same kind of virtual care an *e-visit*. From January 1, 2010 to May 1, 2011, Mehrotra et al. (2013) studied urinary tract and sinus infections using electronic means. They found patients were satisfied with the virtual visits and uncovered two interesting facts. Patients who were provided care through e-visits received more antibiotic prescriptions than those with face-to-face visits; however, the face-to-face patients had more diagnostic tests performed. One concern is that the e-visit patients experienced less follow-up visits (Penn Medicine 2012).

Cincinnati Children's physicians provide *econsults* by using telemedicine technology to review records, images, and to talk with and see the patient. Then, they provide their specialized opinion to physicians in the Caribbean, Dominican Republic, and China. Actually, they possess the capability to provide this service to anyone, anywhere in the world (Brunsman 2014).

Many of these technologies and themes converge. For instance, patient engagement often starts with providing education to a patient about the disease and then providing information on how he or she can actively manage the disease.

Patients can monitor how they feel, what causes changes in their condition, and they can adjust medications based on responses they can monitor through various apps.

Health systems like Intermountain and Cleveland Clinic provide apps they develop for their patients. Cleveland Clinic developed an app for patients with epilepsy. The patients wanted reliable, accurate information, and wanted to understand their condition. An epilepsy physician, Imad Najm, M.D., developed an app that contains information, anatomical models, and the ability to track patients' experiences with seizures for both efficacy of their medications and identification of pre-seizure alerts. This program was so successful that the Cleveland Clinic engaged its 43,000 employees to work on other apps, which they continue to modify to meet patients' needs (Gregg 2014a).

The term *telehealth* evolved to *telecare*. Telehealth included the change from in-person care to virtual care using technology, which focused on the platform for delivering virtual care. The term *telecare* demonstrates that the advancements of technology must include the quality and integrity of the care. Telehealth came about based on patient access needs; however, telecare is instead a proactive approach. New services for online care include a multidisciplinary approach available 24/7 via online access, especially important during transitions from acute care to post-acute care (Andrews 2014).

eHealth

Researchers found that adults rarely use eHealth. In fact, only 17.6% buy medicine online, 19% track their health, and/or e-mail their providers. Older, adult males use eHealth the least. Adults between 18 and 34 are twice as likely to e-mail their provider or search health information online, which creates a digital divide. Those adults with less than a high school education were the least likely to use eHealth.

Individuals who participate in eHealth are the most likely to take charge of their own health status (Kontos, Blake, Chou, and Prestin 2014).

Conclusion

These technologies connect patients to caregivers in real time and change the delivery of healthcare. The change coincides with the Affordable Care Act that contains a tenet that patients take responsibility for their own health. As they take on this accountability, the relationship between patient and provider changes from one of paternalism to one of collegiality where patients know, understand, monitor, and make decisions that affect their health status.

Discussion Questions

1. What are the top clinical and financial benefits of telehealth?
2. How receptive is today's patient to the telemedicine process, and in what ways can he or she engage with the change in delivery models?
3. How are employers and insurers optimizing "virtual care" to achieve positive clinical outcomes?

Assignment

Create a 25-slide PowerPoint presentation with speaker notes describing how leading organizations are effectively engaging patients in prevention measures to reduce hospital readmissions. Include a discussion on the most cutting-edge telemedicine strategies for improving the ease and reducing the cost of chronic patient care. In addition, justify how payors and providers can work in partnership to optimize diabetes care management.

Chapter 2

The Role of mHealth for Self-Care and Remote Care

mHealth refers to the ability to monitor oneself or for a provider to monitor a patient through a mobile device. Mobile technology allows a physician access to important information on the patient's medical record, access to expert information, and the ability to monitor the patient in real time. Additionally, a physician can do it from anywhere. In 2013, there were over 1 million mobile device applications and they continue to grow (Chouffani 2013a).

From 2011 to 2013, mHealth apps moved into the commercialization phase of the market. mHealth app publishers primarily focus on chronically ill patients (31%) and on people's fitness interests (28%). The first users and those considered to be primary users are physicians, who are the specific target for app developers at 14%. In the future, developers will target remote monitoring (53%) and consultation apps (38%) (Research2guidance 2014).

All of this collected data created a move to cloud storage for large repositories of data that were created through continual monitoring. These repositories provide quick access to a patient's medical history, diagnoses, allergies, and other important data needed by clinicians treating patients in urgent and emergent situations. They can see test results and imaging pictures.

mHealth programs might be specifically developed applications for a smartphone or tablet or used in conjunction with FaceTime or Skype, which makes it an adjunct for telehealth. Healthcare consumers use asynchronous access to information and want that same convenience when it comes to healthcare. They like looking up their own information and accessing experts only when necessary. The baby boomer generation especially likes taking charge of their healthcare just as they have taken charge of other aspects of their lives.

In 2013, there were 95 million Americans using mHealth technologies, which represented a 27% growth in just one year. A poll of 8,600 smartphone users found that 38% find their health and medical information through the use of their smartphones. The patient populations who use this technique the most are those with cystic fibrosis, patients with ACNE (growth hormone deficiency), hepatitis C, and Attention Deficit Hyperactivity Deficit (ADHD) along with those diagnosed with Crohn's and migraines (McCann 2013).

Accountable Care Organizations (ACOs) provide coordinated care for patients across all the disciplines needed to help them with optimal health. The commercial sector that ensures the employed population and their dependents were the first covered by ACOs. The next segment was the Medicare ACOs that benefitted from mHealth for concentrated efforts in chronic disease management tools along with reminders and alerts to avoid readmissions to the hospital. Due to the success with the Medicare population and employed population, the experience will be similar in the Medicaid population (Hodge 2014).

Another study shows that 70% of young Americans, 18–34 years old, admitted they postponed visiting a physician because it was not convenient. Of the 2,061 survey participants older than 18 years, 54% reported they also delayed a visit due to inconvenience. The working population finds it difficult to take off from work. They want and need convenience. Interestingly enough, 27% stated they would forego something of value if they could always access a doctor via a mobile device. They see mHealth and telehealth as convenience that eliminates wait times while providing access any time of the day or night. They want access to their own medical records. They do not want to give up quality; instead, they want board certified physicians. They also want timely communication from their physicians (Wicklund 2014e).

Companies also make apps for physician-to-physician communication. For years, physicians used evidence-based medicine, meaning they used scientifically studied treatments for patients. What used to be called *hallway consults*, when one physician stopped another to ask for advice, are now possible through an mHealth app. At the bedside, a physician can seek advice from others from SharePractice (Wicklund 2014b). The physicians use a secure site to write symptoms, test results and problems in order to obtain information, advice, and consults from anyone responding. Physicians are responding to each other and providing clinically proven advice, which can be used right at the patient's bedside (Figure 2.1).

Another new service called *@Point of Care* pulls together information on 15 chronic conditions and provides management and diagnosis based on population sample statistics for physician use at the bedside. These summaries would otherwise take 12 hours of reading by the physician to obtain the same information. Additionally, @Point of Care allows the patient to enter data to update their personal health profile. Another app, Docphin, provides data from 5,000 journals. The site uses an algorithm to select articles most cited about a chronic disease. The algorithm continually updates the information (Schwartz 2014b).

Diabetes commonly affects the elderly, who often live alone in isolation without support from others. Given the isolation, mHealth tools can fill this gap and engage the patient by delivering information while they actively test their blood sugar

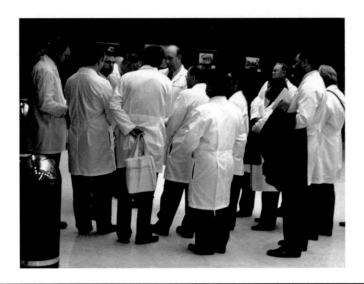

Figure 2.1 Physicians learn about latest technology. (From *Smart Planet* 21, 2014, http://www.smartplanet.com/blog/bulletin/sharepractice-crowdsourcing-wisdom-for-doctors/.)

levels. The app can also deliver education about diet, exercises, health reminders, community resources, and local healthcare providers. In addition, the resources may connect these lonely seniors to online communities of people their own age, living alone, and dealing with diabetes (Javitt 2014). Support from others encourages the elderly to eat right and exercise, which helps to maintain normal flora in the body.

Like other discoveries about the importance of normal flora and the problem caused by abnormal flora, diabetes sufferers possess crAssphage, a virus, found in patients with diabetes and obesity. This virus attaches itself to Bacteroidetes found at the end of the intestinal tract. Initial research shows that its significance lies in how it affects obesity (Diabetes News 2014).

Elder Care

App development for the elderly lags behind apps for all other age groups. Yet, research shows that apps can stimulate the mind and help Alzheimer's patients and others with neuro-logical problems. Scientists have determined that music and art can stimulate the mind. Given this information, GE Health developed apps that stimulate the mind through music and art (Baum 2014c). Nursing homes and assisted living centers use music therapy to stimulate these patients and to engage them in the real world. Playing music familiar to the patient stimulates memory and thinking.

Family members who place their elderly loved ones into an assisted living facility often want to ensure that they receive good, quality care. At the same time, assisted living facilities need to document the care. To meet both needs, CareMerge, an mHealth app, provides a documentation system that fits the government's requirements and informs the family about the care provided at the time it is delivered (Wicklund 2014i).

Many mHealth applications provide vital sign monitoring; however, few monitor activity. Most people follow the same routines daily, especially the elderly. CarePredict tracks movement, location, and motion aggregating it into 7-day patterns. Alerts are sent when patterns change. This monitoring is especially important in Alzheimer's patients who have a tendency to wander and not know where they are going (Wicklund 2014h).

Seniors look for socialization and communication along with the ability to manage their own appointments and health data. Companies that provide this kind of service include Numera, Independa, eCaring, BeClose, and VideoCare.

mHealth provides the data to the patient continuously and may or may not be sent immediately to the provider. Many factors influence the decision for sending or accessing the data. With the use of asynchronous monitoring, providers can batch their time and look up data more efficiently. The access may also include alerts only to significant changes. Then, the system automatically uses algorithms to create evidence-based protocols specific to the patient's needs. These providers review data, diagnose, and treat without the need for administrative, time-consuming tasks, which increases their productivity (Lovrien et al. 2013).

The payors hold hospitals accountable for patients for 30 days post-discharge. In addition, the Patient Protection and Affordable Care Act requires providers to maintain and improve the health of the population. In order to meet the goal of no readmission in 30 days and to keep patients in their optimum healthy state, mHealth monitoring is necessary. A patient may receive a prescription for mHealth devices that monitor blood pressure, temperature (thermometers), oxygenation (pulse oximeters), weight (scales), and spectrometers. These devices gather data and send it to the provider for monitoring and intervention. Research identified potential savings from remote monitoring at $36 billion between 2013 and 2018 (Cox 2013). The global mHealth market predictions for 2018 are $21.5 billion with a compounded annual growth rate of 55% (AuntMinnie 2014).

People know when they are stressed, but often try to discount it. A new app developed by an endocrinologist and a clinical engineer at the University of Utah provides an easy way for anyone to test their stress hormone, cortisol. They use a straw-like device to collect saliva from under the tongue and put the saliva into a reader connected to their smartphone. The results come back instantly. It can validate how people feel and provide them with permission to take a break. In fact, people with psychotic depression often have a spike in their cortisol level just before the depression occurs. An intervention at this point can prevent the depression. The cost of the test is about $5 compared to $50 at a lab with a delay of about 5 days for the results (Janeczko 2014).

Physicians see mHealth as a way to engage the patient in their own health improvement choices. mHealth devices can monitor the patient's condition and send it through a mechanism that interprets the data. Then, these devices use gamification strategies to motivate the patient to make healthy lifestyle choices. Some people think they will become as addicted to gaming health activities as they are to Facebook. Of course, they will still need direction and oversight from providers. The long-term goal focuses on patients taking responsibility for their own health status. The plan includes gamification, social media, and the use of biometric sharing (Wicklund 2014i). Developers think that computer gaming design and technology when used with long distance and mobile applications will reduce healthcare costs by motivating patient participation (Schwartz 2014c).

One of the other issues in elder care involves pain management. People often suffer from chronic pain or intense pain related to cancer during their final years. Pain management can take many forms and one of them is diversion. Oculus Rift provides a virtual reality experience that allows escapism for people suffering from pain and severe, crippling limitations. The 3D experience makes everything appear real whether it is visually watching butterflies or hiking through a mountain pass (Rudderham 2014) (Figure 2.2).

Figure 2.2   Virtual reality can divert attention away from pain. (From Oculus Rift, Oculus VR®, 2014, http://www.oculusvr.com/rift/.)

Self-Monitoring

As patients engage in their health status and maintenance, they will use more mHealth applications for self-testing. They continue to adopt these applications without consulting or sharing the results with their physicians. In fact, most physicians do not think usage will change patient behavior. These physicians disregard the evidence that diabetic patients live longer with fewer complications than they did prior to self-testing and monitoring. Further evidence shows that patients do purchase these apps; the industry grew by 19% as evidenced by products at the App Store (Mobiquity 2014) (Figure 2.3).

By mid-2014, Apple's App Store contained 15,000 health and fitness apps, of which only 120 received U.S. Food and Drug Administration (FDA) approval (Flaherty 2014). During the first half of 2014, consumers increased their health and fitness apps by 62%; however, other apps only grew at 33%, which means that fitness apps grew 87% faster than the others. The fitness app users spend triple the time using their apps compared to nonfitness app users with a population comprised of 62% women and 38% men. The age group using the fitness apps the most are between 35 and 44 years old (47%), followed by the 25–24 year olds (41%), with 35% of the total as runners (Jayanthi 2014a).

The Nike and iPod fitness app contains an accelerator. It measures the acceleration by gravity or movement. The sensor is in the shoe and it transmits a message to the app allowing the user to monitor progress. The combination of GPS and accelerator are rated as good components. Fitness experts also suggest a connection to social media for encouragement. The user needs to decide how much digital information they want others to know about them (Kahn 2014).

Every day, insurers, providers, and developers look for more ways to engage patients in monitoring their own parameters. iPatientCare, a medical informatics company, developed

Figure 2.3   Use of health and fitness apps. (From Mobiquity, 2014, http://www.mobiquityinc.com.)

three apps to help patients monitor medication compliance called *miMeds*. Another app, MiCalc was designed for pregnant mothers to help them take better care of themselves and in turn deliver healthier babies. The app calculates body mass index, ideal body weight, body surface area, and due date. It also helps pregnant women limit weight gain, which is good for them and good for the baby. The miWater app keeps track of the amount of water intake a day and sends an alert if the patient is not drinking enough water. Every time an individual drinks a cup of water, it is entered into the app (Brandt 2014).

As mHealth and associated apps gain mainstream use, the benefits include more patient engagement. In addition, providers access the data and information they need no matter where they are without limitations based on the time of day. With the ease of access, Health Insurance Portability and Accountability Act (HIPAA) concerns increase because the data can easily be hacked for fraudulent use. The issues center on the fact that more nonhealthcare developers enter the medical and fitness app market segment. Increasingly, Google Glass interfaces with apps (Jayanthi 2014b). No one has addressed what it means for patient privacy.

Google X worked with Novartis to develop a smart lens that can monitor body fluids and also adjust vision by autofocusing. The idea is to help patients self-monitor and also to restore normal function. Each smart lens contains a wireless microchip that can sense glucose levels and transmit that data to another device. The device records a reading every second. Researchers state that they will probably add an LED warning system that can alert the wearer to either a high or low glucose reading that will allow the wearer to take appropriate action before a problem occurs. Google X has other products in development; however, they are pretty secretive about them. Almost 400 million people, or 1 in every 19, currently has some form of diabetes, which equates to 29 million people in the United States or almost 10% (Bennett 2014). These new products indicate Google's interest in moving into the healthcare market with emerging technologies to serve those suffering from diabetes and other diseases.

Google X also announced the development of a human body project that connects 100 medical experts whose focus is on biochemistry, physiology, imaging, and molecular biology, plus optics. These scientists are connected by a computer network that will collect their data to analyze normal and abnormal body functions at the cellular level in an effort to identify natural disease prevention (Barr 2014).

The trend of self-monitoring began with glucometers in the 1990s, and recent studies show that while the incidence of diabetes has increased by 50% over the past 20 years, the amputation rate has declined by 50%. As patients began to monitor their own blood sugar levels accurately, they were more likely to keep them in a range that created fewer complications from the disease (CDC 2014). This progress shows that the more patients engage in their own health status, the more likely they are to increase their own quality of life.

New products for controlling blood sugar include both glucose monitoring devices like BG5, which morphed into BF1, designed in white with a sleek compact look that fits with an iPhone's design. A tear-drop-shaped meter fits into the headphone jack of an Apple or Android smartphone. Like traditional glucometers, a drop of blood on a test strip is inserted into the device and the reading shows on the smartphone (Sullivan 2014a).

In conjunction with glucose monitoring, insulin pumps (OmniPod) no longer require implantation into the body. Small reservoirs, the size of a quarter, can be adhered to the skin, and insulin is pumped into the system without the use of needles (OmniPod.com) (Figure 2.4).

In cases of body fluid analysis, many currently involve the use of test strips that change color according to the test results. Patients first used test strips that changed color to indicate a result and they compared the result against a table to determine what the result meant; however, a better and

The OmniPod
advances insulin pump
therapy. **Again.**

Learn more ›

Figure 2.4   The OmniPod is a tubeless insulin pump system made by Insulet Corporation. It has just two parts: the Pod and the PDM (Personal Diabetes Manager). The small Pod has the reservoir, infusion set, automated inserter, pumping mechanism, and power supply built in. It is adhered directly to the skin and insulin is delivered without the need for multiple daily injections. The handheld PDM controls insulin delivery to the Pod, calculates suggested doses, and insulin onboard, and has a built-in blood glucose meter (http://www.myomnipod.com).

more accurate method comes from laboratory equipment using spectrometry. Recently, however, newer tests show good accuracy in reading these test strips. In order to ensure accuracy, ColorMetrix created an app that uses the camera in a smartphone combined with an algorithm to convert data from the colorimetric into a numerical value (concentration), which takes seconds to perform. The result can be saved on the phone and/or sent to a healthcare professional who also reviews the test results (S. Collins 2014) (Figure 2.5).

Cue developed (Wasserman 2014) a product that uses color cartridges to detect biomarkers for inflammation, testosterone, fertility, and vitamin D. Home users collect the fluid using a white test strip that they insert into a microfluidic-filled cartridge, the tabletop analyzer then performs the analysis and displays the results on the iPhone through the use of an app. The popularity of Cue derives from the fact that it delivers data that interests both the physician and the patient. Cue focuses on test results that patients and physicians need to determine health status. Once patients understand their test results, they then want a dialogue with their physician about what they should do about the results (Wicklund 2014b) (Figure 2.6).

Figure 2.5 Self-testing devices for laboratory analysis at home. (From Yetisen, Ali, University of Cambridge, United Kingdom, 2014, http://www.cam.ac.uk/research/news/pocket-diagnosis.)

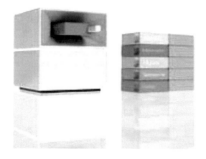

Figure 2.6 At-home lab testing. (Courtesy of Cue. From Fierce Medical Devices, 2014, http://www.fiercemedicaldevices.com/story/mobile-medical-app-brings-laboratory-testing-home/2014-06-12.)

In 2014, the FDA approved an app that monitors atrial fibrillation and sends the report to the patient. Previously, the tracing was sent to a physician who read and interpreted the report and then notified the patient. The accuracy of the computer read tracing led the FDA to send the report directly to the patient. The wireless monitoring device snaps onto an iPhone and creates a single lead tracing of the heart rhythm (Saxena 2014c).

Other tests and data are more simplistic. For instance, diners can use an app to scan their dinner and the service from TellSpec analyzes the food and sends back information. If the diner is worried about food allergies, the contents are readily reviewed and sent to the diner to use to avoid eating allergenic food. TellSpec quickly identify allergens, calories, chemicals, nutrients, and other ingredients present in the scanned food. These findings are then sent to a TellSpec app on the user's device (Bertolucci 2014).

Complex tests that required a visit to an outpatient clinic or a physician's office include analyzing mood and lung function. A new application for the smartphone detecting the rate, flow, and depth of breathing can indicate lung capacity and function, while the tone, inflection, volume, rhythm, and rapidity of speech can detect the mood of the individual. The voice actually identifies mood and anxiety levels; however, the interpretation was qualitative until now. A new application can actually quantify it and rate the problem (Topol 2014).

People already diagnosed with a mental disorder like bipolar disease, post-traumatic stress disorder, and Parkinson's disease can also benefit from an app that monitors breathing and voice. The app runs in the background and analyzes the voice during conversations on the phone. The app contains an algorithm that analyzes and correlates speech patterns to a person's mood. No one hears the conversation; the app just performs the analysis to identify mood shifts for early intervention (Melnick 2014).

In addition, the data entered by patients, data sent from monitors, and analysis of passive data such as that entered on Twitter and Facebook can help providers obtain a more comprehensive picture of a patient's mood or an alteration in mood. Software, like Ginger.io, collects and analyzes data input from the phone. It flags changes relative to patient mood and sends an alert to a provider or case manager providing an opportunity for early intervention (Chouffani 2013b).

People often want to improve their health status and perform self-analysis and monitoring. For instance, the ZEO headband monitors the depth and length of sleep of the user. One can wear the headband while experimenting on increasing the quality and length of sleep. A wearer might change the lighting in the room, take magnesium supplements, or limit caffeine and alcohol. If each change is done independently, the data from ZEO shows which interventions increased the depth and length of the sleep. This self-analysis is known as the *Quantified Self.* Many individuals prefer to avoid costly physician visits and like to experiment on their own. Athletes typically work with a trainer to monitor their activities. The qualifiable self is just an extension of the same work without the use of the trainer (*The Economist* 2014).

Wearable Devices

The fitness craze spawned the development of wearable devices to monitor energy expenditures and other parameters used to determine fitness. The Vitality Group conducted a 3-year study to determine the effectiveness of these devices. Those who were not previously participating in fitness activities and adopted the use of these devices decreased their risk factors by 13% while those who were already engaged reduced their factors by 22%. Interestingly enough, the use of devices falls into age groups. Those using a pedometer are in the 35–44 age bracket, while those who use smartphone apps fall into the 18–34 age bracket (Cook 2014).

Another study reviewed those who use health and fitness apps the most, which is the middle-aged (25–54) woman. They used these apps three times more often than others and comprised 62% of the users. The fitness apps grew 87% faster than other apps (Russell 2014).

Researchers found that those who used the fitness tracker were obese and that the use helped them achieve an improvement in fitness and those who used a fitness tracker combined with a wellness program enjoyed the biggest improvement. Physicians at Massachusetts General used Fitbit to help their obese patients increase their exercise habits. These patients received texts containing encouragement and also tips about how to exercise when the weather was bad. Many of these patients suffered from diabetes due to their weight. Those who used the tracker and who also received the texts did a better job of controlling their blood sugar (Dowskin and Walker 2014).

Mayo Clinic physicians used Fitbit to track and encourage post open-heart patients to move. Their study showed that patients who moved the most on their first post-op day had shorter lengths-of-stay and more improved function. If the patient was not moving, an alert was sent to the physical therapist to visit and assist the patient to improve and increase his or her mobility (Dowskin and Walker 2014).

Gartner reports that more than 2,000 wellness programs also incorporated the fitness tracking device. Of the users, 86% stated that using the device motivated them to move more (Dowskin and Walker 2014).

Appirio provided 400 Fitbits to their employees and watched them improve their health status. In fact, it was so improved that they showed the data to their insurance carrier and was able to reduce their premiums by 5%, which amounted to a $280,000 savings. The employees were not required to share their data; however, 100 of them did share it. Most were fine with sharing their exercise information, but chose not to share their sleep habits. Fitbit gave the insurance company $20,000 to privately start a wellness program and they in turn awarded exercise bands to the employees (Bort 2014).

Since insurance companies have the most to gain from fitness tracking mechanisms, it makes sense that they have the best history and experience with them. In 2013, people spent $1.6 billion on these devices and researchers predict the number will increase to $5 billion in 2016. Aetna subscribers can direct their Jawbone or Fitbit device to send the data directly to them for inclusion in their profile (Boulton 2014b).

The challenge is that most people like the novelty of the fitness app, but the novelty wears off after 6 months and few use them longer than this amount of time. The other problem is that the market is flooded with various apps creating stiff competition. Research shows that future success depends on the ability to diversify the apps and to develop wearable clothing, wristbands, and headbands for specific needs. Competition requires more sophisticated tools.

Another product, OMsignal, contains sensors for heart rate, calories burned, and breathing, all contained in a wearable shirt. The sensors send data to a mobile app. The material contains antimicrobial material using spandex and polyester. The product can be machine washed, but not dried. The sensor threads in the clothing send the data to a clip-on receiver that transmits the data to the cloud, where it is parsed and analyzed. AiQ Smart Clothing and Hexoskin are the chief competitors of OMsignal (Rosman 2014).

After these initial gadgets were developed, the medical device industry started to look at Bluetooth technology that could send physiological data to providers for use. The center of this advancement was the smartphone with predictions that the smart watch will move into that same space. Wearable devices were first designed for a single function, were difficult to connect to anything else, and were known as "dumb devices" (Tabuchi 2013). ABI Research (2013) predicts that by 2017, wearable fitness devices will reach 90 million units. That number signifies a 41% growth rate from 2011 to 2017.

As the incidence of skin cancer continues to increase, many people use sunscreen, and UV-preventative clothing to protect themselves. Another wearable device, the Netatmo June bracelet, actually monitors the UV rays on the skin and sends a message to the wearer's phone to alert him or her to apply more sunscreen or sunblock. The good thing about this bracelet is that it reminds the wearer during windy and chilly weather when people often forget about the exposure to sunrays. The device incorporated the guidelines from the World Health Organization specific to the wearers' skin type. The one drawback is that the device is not waterproof (Stern 2014).

New start-up companies and established medical device companies recognized the potential in using wearable devices to monitor the physiology levels in the body. For instance, Samsung launched a $50 million venture firm for the sole purpose of creating wearable technology. The Simband wearable hardware platform (wristband sensor for continuous monitoring) combined with SAMI (Samsung Architecture for Multimodal Interactions) open software (Samsung) is making this technology available to developers (Sarvastani 2014).

Premature babies often leave the hospital with critical needs for continued monitoring. The first baby monitor provided sound so that parents would know when the baby was awake. Some went home with an oxygen monitor with an alarm that sounded if the oxygen saturation was lower than 90. Subsequently, Kurt Colvin invented a smart sock for babies that monitors oxygen levels, heart rate, skin temperature, sleep position, quality of sleep, and the position along with skin temperature and rollover alerts. These alerts are sent to a parent's smartphone for immediate attention (Owlet 2013).

Scientists also developed a heartbeat monitor that can evaluate the beat from across the house without the use of sensors placed on the baby or in the room. Instead, it uses WiFi signals that track the rise and fall of the chest at 99% accuracy. This monitor can track four people at a time (Brewster 2014).

Another device created for babies is moving into the adult world. Premature babies require monitoring of their urine. Scientists developed a diaper with sensors that analyze nutrition, hydration, and type 1 diabetes. In the adult world, there is also a need to track urinary tract infections, which are common in nursing home and dementia patients. The research noted that the market potential for the Pixie Briefs is $6 billion a year since there are 5 million people with dementia who suffer from incontinence and acquire chronic urinary tract infections. In addition, 500,000 preterm babies could benefit from this kind of tracking (Combs 2014).

Children provide unique challenges for diagnostic reasons. They often possess limited language skills. Gaming is one way to test their abilities and to diagnose deficits. One in four children are born with a lazy eye and if not properly treated by the age of 9, their vision deteriorates in that eye. Therefore, ophthalmologists devised a game that tests visual acuity, depth perception, and color identification (Wicklund 2014m).

Children frequently suffer from ear infections. Parents face choices when deciding to seek care for possible infections. They can make an appointment, which often conflicts with other activities, and creates a delay, or they can take the child to an urgent care or emergency department for diagnosis and treatment. A new attachment, CellScope Oto, for the iPhone allows it to function like an otoscope. The device fits over the camera on the phone and allows the parent to take a picture of the eardrum. A small plastic speculum is placed in the outer opening of the ear where the parent can take a picture to send to a physician for diagnosis and a treatment plan. Insurance does not cover the diagnosis and treatment, but the cost is often the same as the out-of-pocket cost (copay) of seeing a physician. Parents like the convenience and quick interaction (Carnns 2014).

These devices are moving into the realm of sending alerts to the patient to correct their body mechanics. For instance, the most common cause of backaches is poor posture, which costs $50 billion in healthcare dollars every year. Now, patients can wear a belt that monitors posture and alerts them to stand and sit up straight. Biomechanical monitoring tracks how sedentary or active the patient is and alerts them to get up and move, to correct posture, and to address a myriad of other things including the quality of their sleep (Rowe 2013).

People who suffer seizures often have subtle warnings just prior to a seizure and know what to expect; however, some people do not recognize any warning signals. A new wearable device contains a thermometer, hydration sensor, accelerometer, pressure sensors, pulse oximeter, and a microphone. It connects through Bluetooth to communicate the sensors' readings to the individual's smartphone app. The sensors begin to identify patterns about what triggers a threshold and at what level it occurs. The warning allows the wearer to get to a safe place and call for help with an automated 911 call before the seizure occurs (Pogoreic 2014a).

Many of the pains people suffer are actually induced by some bad habits. Most people work on a computer, hunched over a keyboard for the computer in an ergonomically incorrect position that causes long-term problems. A circular wearable device helps people improve their posture when sitting at the computer. It is 2.5 cm in diameter and 9 mm in thickness. It sends alerts to an app on the individual's smartphone when his or her posture is not appropriate. These reminders help individuals avoid long-term damage to the spine through improper posture (Soo 2014).

Another costly risk involves seniors admitted to hospitals who become disoriented and often fall causing injury to themselves. Another wearable sensor, Zephyr BioModule, tracks patients' skin temperature, heart rate, physical activity, and EKG. This tracking provides data for predictive analytics where data becomes an algorithm used to estimate fall risk (Pecci 2014).

Patient Engagement

All of these mHealth applications add some convenience for patients. They use apps every day to find the nearest location of a service, schedule an appointment, find out the cost, and how the service is rated. Most healthcare entities have failed to use these apps to gain market share, trust, or loyalty. Since it is a part of everyday life, more apps that help the patient find services, ratings, and pricing are needed since patients bear more of the out-of-pocket costs than they did in the past and that has spiked their interest in ratings and pricing (Slepin 2014).

Researchers have identified the changing patterns used by patients to find a physician; 77% have used the Internet to search for a physician and/or hospital; most performed this search over a 2-week period prior to making the decision; 56% called for an appointment via the phone, 21% booked an appointment online, only 23% booked in person. As more health systems provide the opportunity to book appointments on their own, this growth will continue. After the appointment, 12% posted something about their experience online. The majority (57%) of searches online were to find information about health (Google Research 2012).

Mayo Clinic and Kaiser Permanente provide a patient app that allows patients to securely e-mail their physicians and to make or cancel their own appointments, review their own test results and medical records, and obtain refills for their medications. Kaiser also has an app that tracks walking for fitness and another one helps patients keep track of their flex spending account balance (Pai 2014).

Obamacare changes the delivery of care and requires good information from patients along with engagement in maintaining and improving their own health status. The most likely way to obtain accurate patient information comes from familiar patient behavior such as using a smartphone. PriceWaterhouse researchers determined that Europeans could save 35% on healthcare costs through the use of mHealth technologies. This figure applied to the U.S. healthcare cost savings in U.S. dollars equals $700 billion (Freedman 2014).

Patient engagement can create customer loyalty. If the patient seeks all health information online at their provider's Web site, they will use the services found there. With the focus on engagement, Altarum developed an assessment guide they call *ACE* (Altarum Consumer Engagement), which is a survey tool used to measure four domains of engagement that identifies how a person's behavior affects an individual's health and healthcare. The outcome of the survey determines the four elements of engagement: ownership, commitment, informed choice, and navigation (Lynch 2014).

One of the keys to successful recovery and prevention in cardiac care is to engage the patient in healthy behaviors that include diet and exercise. Research over the past 20 years has shown that patients who engage in cardiac rehab experience a 45% reduction in mortality at 5 years post-intervention; however, some patients cannot participate due to lack of transportation to the program. These patients receive a new app, Wellframe, which is installed on their smartphone. They receive a daily list of things to do along with a log for documenting their exercise, and reminders to take their medication (Brimmer 2014).

Community health centers traditionally care for low-income patients who have fewer options for care. They also historically fail to adhere to their treatment plan. A planned intervention used computerized reminders in the form of e-mail, text, and phone reminders for patients who were required to conduct a home fecal immunochemical test. These methods have improved compliance from 37 to 82% (Baker et al. 2014).

Health-enabling technologies (HET) involve the use of both information and communication technologies that engage patients and empower them to make healthy choices. These technologies augment the interaction patients had with professionals, extend their engagement, and increase the chances to manage chronic disease processes. The strengths of HET center on portability, data collection, adaptability, and increased communication between providers and patients. Stanford University researchers developed an Internet program that provides information to patients on self-management based on their diagnosis. The Internet program works well alone or in combination with apps to support self-management (Knight and Shea 2014).

Merck Medical Information and Innovation (M2i2) created an online community called *PatientsLikeMe*. It had 250,000 users by mid-2014. The site provides advanced research information and connects patients with similar diseases who can share their experiences, advice, and resource knowledge together. In the beginning, Merck hoped that they could obtain more specific data on patients using certain drugs and the outcomes; however, they found it difficult to obtain the specific data that met the requirements for scientific data collection. Next, they decided to structure the data collection, which produced usable results. The results of this online community showed that patients connected with each other first and secondarily provided credible and usable information (Jain 2014).

HET creates a connection between providers and patients that did not exist previously. The first concern for connectedness focused on interoperability, meaning that the software used by one provider must connect seamlessly to the software used by another provider. Physicians shared the patient's medical problems, longitudinal risks, previous treatments, and interventions. Once providers started sharing data and connecting with each other, they noted that patient compliance to the treatment plan was just as important as connecting to each other. They termed this connection as *patient engagement.* Social media and gamification help patients obtain a deeper understanding of their diagnosis and treatment along with the rationale behind the treatment plan and the importance of complying with the plan or contacting the provider if problems arise with the treatment plan.

In order to deliver value-based care as described in the Obamacare legislation, physicians and healthcare leaders need accurate information. Redundancy and inappropriate visits to the wrong provider increase the cost of care. For this reason, Lanier developed an app that helps patients provide accurate information needed to triage these patients to the appropriate healthcare provider: physician, dietitian, physical therapist, or other healthcare discipline (Freedman 2014).

Another study determined that patients were more forthcoming and accurate in providing information when they perceived reporting to a computer rather than an individual. They fear judgment from another human that they do not fear from a computer.

Software companies provide interactions and follow up with patients to track progress and lack of engagement. For instance, EmmiPrevent was designed to stimulate health activity by the patient. Summa Health Network noted a 24% increase in diabetic patient follow-up and a 13% improvement in their (Health Effectiveness Data and Information Set) HEDIS score through the use of this software (Emmi Solutions 2014). HEDIS is a national indicator regarding the effectiveness of care patients receive.

Voxiva received endorsement from CMS for their preventative programs for mothers and children, adult health and wellness (Txt4health), smoking cessation (Text2Quit), and diabetes self-management (Care4life Diabetes). These programs engage the patient by providing text messages that stimulate wellness behaviors (Slabodkin 2014a).

In addition to the apps, many individuals search online for their own diagnosis. The breakdown on who uses this access is interesting. Women traditionally take charge of their health. So, it is no wonder that they check online more often than men. They try to find their own diagnosis before consulting a physician. Pew Research (Fox and Duggan 2013) shows that young, highly educated, white adults with incomes >\$75,000 are the most likely to look online.

The secret to managing the health of a population requires focused interventions and dialogue with patients. EmmiPrevent is a voice-activated service designed with specific information for targeted patients. The software responds to answers from the patient and collects data that is automatically entered into the patient's chart. Information delivered matches the patient's needs. A study of 289 patients engaged in this service showed that EmmiPrevent call campaigns achieved a 13% HEDIS (Healthcare Effectiveness Data and Information Set) score improvement within 6 weeks. The service was able to confirm appointments for eye exams in 43% of the patients and, in addition, it transferred 3% of the patients to a scheduler for an appointment with their primary care physician (Emmi Solutions 2014).

Another software designed to help providers engage patients is called *Scriplogix*, which focuses on the use of behavioral techniques, analytics, and technology to identify patient preferences to actively motivate patients to follow their care plan. The analytics provides information that profiles patients according to their risk factors by combing through their medical history, demographics, and other social factors. Next, the patients are segmented by motivation and ability, which identifies motivational triggers based on their characteristics. The progress is measured and delivered via dashboard to the provider or case manager. The program is designed for risk identification and stratification allowing for segmentation through profiling patient activation and patient engagement. The analysis uses social media and sentiment analytics and includes both structured and unstructured data. The data on readmission to acute care and medication adherence identifies which patients require more intensive case management. Early detection of chronic disease promotes case management and optimal health status. It can also follow up on any hospital-acquired condition and identify triggers to promote prevention. All of these techniques decrease healthcare spending (Scriplogix 2014).

Researchers at the University of North Carolina at Chapel Hill demonstrated that other Web-based interventions can also improve health and mitigate the development of predisposed disease conditions. Instead of one-on-one visits between a patient and a healthcare provider, live Web-based sessions via group counseling demonstrated effectiveness in preventing the onset of heart disease. The Framingham Risk Score that predicts the development of future heart disease was reduced through the use of the Web-based program. Twelve months following the initiation of the program, enrolled patients showed lower blood pressure and blood cholesterol levels, improved diet, increased physical activity, and adherence to their prescribed medication (Goth 2014g).

In a survey of healthcare leaders, 59% noted that patient engagement was their top challenge. Of these leaders, 78% acknowledged that nurse phone calls were the most effective method of creating patient engagement and the only one that ranked higher than 40% of all their tactics (Zeis 2014). No matter what technology is used to connect with patients, they still like the one-on-one relationship.

Since patient engagement relies on technology, many organizations now provide direction to patients on apps and Web sites that present credible and reliable information. Ochsner Clinic just launched O Bar, which is patterned after Apple's Genius Bar. O Bar is where patients can seek advice and technical help in locating and downloading apps (Weinstock 2014).

Gamification

One of the ways to engage patients comes from gamification, which can take many forms. One form uses video. Pediatricians, Jason Kahn, Katrina Miaoulis, and Alex Rotenberg, developed a video game technology, which provides biofeedback as part of family therapy to reduce the risk for psychosis-related responses (rage) (McCann 2014g).

Gaming also provides education and training to providers. Online gaming improved blood pressure control to patients in a shorter amount of time for physicians who participated in the gaming versus those who did not participate. Gamification uses a technique called *spaced education* where the learner gains information and reinforcement of the information over a period of time (Goth 2014d). This study was conducted by researchers at Harvard University, who think it is the first study using online, educational games to train physicians.

Pennsylvania instituted a program that enters patients into a lottery. Their eligibility depends on compliance to their prescribed medications post-cardiac treatment. The program called *Strong* uses a technology in the cap of the medication bottle. The GlowCap flashes and beeps when patients forget to take their medications. After 3 days of missing the medication, a family member or friend receives an alert to check on the patient to find out why no medication was taken. Researchers note that patients are more likely to comply with their prescription plan if they have an active support network (Ward 2014).

New Accountability

Previously, providers received their reimbursement from a third-party payor. The patient was insulated from costs; however, with the advent of high-deductible plans including those found through the government health exchanges, people bear more responsibility for the payment and want to look for the best price. The Health Research Institute surveyed 1,000 people and found that in addition to the $2.8 trillion spent on healthcare, individuals also spent money on medical products like healthcare games, apps, and rating services.

As people assume responsibility for their care and use online resources, they need accurate information. Most people use keywords and a search engine to find the information they need. No mechanism currently exists to rate the results from this methodology. Kitchens, Harle, and Li (2012) found that health-related search engine queries result in high-quality information. In addition, the quality of information was the same regardless of the ranking; however, preventative and social health searches resulted in a lower quality of results. Due to the variations found in this research, policy makers need to take a look at these sites and engines.

One would think that only the young use the Internet to find information about health and disease; however, the Pew Research Center found that 6 in 10 adults use the Internet and the more affluent and educated the senior, the more they used it. Those over 75 used it less frequently at 37% while 71% of these seniors go online every day and 11% use it three more times per week. These numbers note a 6% year-over-year increase in usage (Smith 2014).

Of those surveyed, many patients want to take charge of both diagnosis and treatment. When asked about using specific apps for teledermatology and monitoring vital signs, 55% reported they would use them. Many like the convenience and 47% like the idea that they can check to see if their child has an ear infection, 44% would perform their own EKG using a smartphone, 42% would do urinalysis, and 39% prefer a telemedicine visit with a provider (Comstock 2014a).

These statistics point to the need to provide good health information in order to improve the health of the population as required in the Affordable Care Act. Reimbursement continues to evolve from care of the ill to care that improves the health of individuals.

Training

High-fidelity simulation labs provide lifelike experiences for healthcare providers to hone their skills. Educators use them for mock trauma, cardiac arrest, delivery, and other emergency situations. Now, these simulation labs also use apps specially designed for first responders to send critical information from the field to the emergency department (Modern Healthcare 2014).

Robotics

New technology includes the use of robots to perform surgery, transfer supplies, provide wayfinding, and a variety of other patient care functions including delivering meals, removing trash, and delivering supplies. Robotic surgical devices steady the hand and allow minimally invasive surgery not possible with the human hand. Many hospitals use a wayfinding app that guides patients and visitors to their location in the parking lot to their destination in the building. Many hospital campuses are large confusing configurations. These wayfinding applications provide step-by-step directions using a GPS that shows where they are and the destination.

Patients interact with a variety of caregivers on any given day. Badges worn by the staff connect to the television in a patient's room. When they walk into a room, the caregiver's name is displayed on the television screen just as incoming calls are shown. It ensures that patients know who they are. The system also tracks who goes in and out of the room. Sometimes, patients and family members think there may not have been much care or interaction during a shift or day. This technology tracks this function (Mace 2014d).

The more that people can function on their own, the healthier they are. People with lower extremity paralysis develop hypertension and blood clots due to the inactivity of these limbs. The FDA approved an exoskeleton device, ReWalk, that makes it possible for people with lower extremity paralysis to walk. It allows them to function better and helps to avoid the health problems associated with inactivity (Baum 2014f).

Other mobility aids for paralyzed victims include Neurobridge that bypasses the spinal cord to connect the brain directly to muscles. It is an electronic neural bypass that allows voluntary and functional control of a paralyzed limb. The system requires an implanted chip in the brain that reads the patient's thought and transmits it to a receiver worn on the impaired limb.

This device allows the limb to function normally as if the spinal cord was still intact and transmitting signals (Ruhe 2014).

Prosthetic feet (Magellan) now include sensors and technology that allows for data capture to fine tune the prosthesis to the patient. A microprocessor in the foot transmits the data, which provides good information used to adjust the foot to the individual wearer. The prosthesis can also adapt to the type of surface the prosthesis encounters. In addition, patients can make adjustments to the angle and height using an app. Patients can continually make adjustments for comfort, stability, and effectiveness (Ruhe 2014).

Changing Payor Practices

One of the most frustrating parts of the U.S. healthcare system is the lack of transparency in the price of care to the patient. Historically, patients were insulated from the charges since most of the bill was paid by the insurance company or the government. Only the employer watched the premiums and cost rise; however, as patients assume more responsibility in paying for their care, they want to know what it costs and why.

Many hospitals cannot quote the cost of a procedure prior to providing the care. Healthcare leaders are more interested now that patients pay more of the bill; therefore, they concentrate on revenue cycle management. In other words, they want the patient to pay their copay upfront. The patients can only make a payment if they know what it is. Therefore, the onus on hospitals is to refine their accounting systems to price out care.

The other pressure comes from changing the reimbursement from volume to value where the government and payors focus on the provider's responsibility to keep people healthy (population health) instead of paying for interventions. Under Obamacare's Accountable Care Organizations, providers receive bundled payments, which they divide among all those associated with the care.

As with other issues in healthcare, there is now an app for that. Cambria developed an app called *Wellero,* which givers providers and consumers a way to access the copay. Wellero sells their app to health insurance companies who ask their subscribers to use it. Everyone benefits since payors, providers, and patients know how much the care will cost and the copay can be collected at the point of service. This copay often accounts to 30% of the total charge. Futurists predict the beginning of a new disruption in payment stemming from the interoperability component of Obamacare (Arrigo 2014).

Conclusion

As the baby boomers age, they could overwhelm the healthcare system or they could change aging and healthcare. Most people want to age in place in their own homes, follow their own habits, and network with friends and family. With the advent of self-monitoring and wearable devices, they might be able to maintain their independence. Baby boomers have wanted to control the direction of their lives from the time they came of age and they continue to demand independence and create new norms for their lifestyle.

Through patient engagement, they can collaborate with physicians to make decisions about their care and to control their treatment plans. Through the use of gamification, they can remain physically and mentally active assuring their independence.

Discussion Questions

1. What is the best way to work with new apps and new attachments for the devices and their applications and integrate them into an organization's daily workflow?
2. As patients become more engaged using mHealth and apps to monitor their health, how will the role of the physician change?

Assignment

mHealth apps and associated devices were designed to provide more information about the patient and to make it accessible to providers and case managers to create timely opportunity for early intervention and to mitigate evolving patient problems before they become more severe. Discuss the best way to work these new devices and applications into an organization's daily workflow. Since it is possible to capture so much data, address how to determine what to keep and what to disregard. In addition, justify how much is needed and when it becomes too much.

Legislation does not match the needs created by the increased data. Propose how to safeguard the data to prevent costly security breaches to prevent HIPAA violations.

Analyze the problems that occur when mHealth devices are not interoperable with one another or network infrastructures. Propose a recommendation to address the problem. In addition to the legislation governing mHealth, organizations like IEEE and the International Organization for Standardizaton (ISO) developed standards and frameworks. For instance, ISO IEEE 11073 developed a group of standards to address personal health device interoperability, connectivity, and data transport. Explain the role physicians can play in providing guidance to manufacturers and system integration to deliver mHealth products that improve patient care in a timely and cost-effective manner.

Chapter 3

Legislation and Trends in Emerging Technologies

In his state of the union message in January of 2004, President Bush laid the foundation to require electronic medical records for the following 10 years. In 2009, President Obama signed into law the American Recovery and Reinvestment Act (ARRA) to stimulate the economy. A provision in ARRA was the Health Information Technology for Economic and Clinical Health Act (HITECH), which included $27 billion over 10 years to induce providers to implement electronic medical records. Physicians who met the guidelines received $18,000 in 2011 for a total of $44,000 through 2013. The electronic record must meet certification criteria (meaningful use) through Medicare in order to qualify for the monies. A slight majority (59%) of providers who are eligible and registered for the federal electronic health record (EHR) incentive program achieved meaningful use and of those 50% of Medicare doctors are at risk for penalties next year under the program. In 2015, entities without electronic records will receive a penalty against their Medicare and Medicaid payments. Stage 2 meaningful use contains 126 requirements: meeting the requirement is all or nothing. Meeting 99% of the requirements does not matter (Manos 2014).

Meaningful use also requires that patients can access their own medical records. As providers set up access for patients, most apps require an e-mail address. For providers working with immigrants, this requirement adds an additional challenge. They first need to convince patients that it is safe to obtain and share an e-mail address. Then, they teach the patient how to use it.

When the Patient Protection and Affordable Care Act was implemented, it included another requirement called *interoperability*, which means medical software must interface with each other. The provider must show that 5% of patients access their own records in order to meet this standard. For New York Hospital Queens, it means 450–500 patients must access their own records during each quarter. Another complication for serving immigrants is that translation of the record into their native language is also required. In a place like New York, this means providing six different languages with five different alphabets (Millard 2014b).

Typically, healthcare technology regulation falls under the U.S. Food and Drug Administration (FDA), which regulates drugs and devices (both those used to treat patients and those used to monitor them); however, currently there are discussions about whether mobile medical applications fall under the FDA or not. While the use of these applications fits within the role of the FDA, the smartphone or tablet they run on does not fall under its purview.

The FDA announced three general categories for classifying information technology products. The first category contains low-risk items in the software realm, which includes billing and coding software and inventory management. The second low-risk category covers medication management, provider order entry, most clinical decision support software, and other health management IT products. The FDA does not intend to provide oversight in this area.

The higher-risk category focuses on medical devices, implants, and clinical monitoring equipment, along with computer-aided detection software used in imaging diagnostics, and radiation treatment software (Health and Human Services 2014b).

As much as scientists and medical researchers focus on the use of genomics to predict and treat an individual's inherited disease, the government still needs to monitor the service, its quality, and the issues. For instance, 23andMe provides genetic information that includes the inherited health lines from an individual's bloodline. In 2014, the FDA barred 23andMe from conducting these genetic tests due to some errors in the results. Subsequently, 23andMe applied for a single health product used to predict a serious, but fairly rare inherited condition called *Bloom Syndrome*, which was approved. The FDA continues its responsibility to approve all genetic testing from every company (Annas and Elias 2014).

Clinical Trials

The government controls clinical trials in order to ensure patient safety and privacy. Clinical trials are costly, hard to manage, and require close scrutiny. One of the issues in recruiting patients is the potential for bias during recruitment. The use of analytics to mine data from electronic records compiles an unbiased sample of patients who meet the criteria for the clinical trial. Then, through the use of mobile technology, adverse event capture occurs in real time with more accuracy (Lee 2014).

Mobile Medical Applications

With the advent of the iPhone and, subsequently, other smartphone devices, programmers developed apps for use by individuals and providers to monitor the health status of an individual. These apps range from simple to complex. At the simplest level, one can simply input the number of calories consumed and the application creates a sum total. On a more complex level, vital signs and other physiologic parameters like heart rhythms are collected and transferred to someone monitoring them at a remote site. As the use increases in complexity, the rationale for oversight from the FDA weighs more heavily on the need for oversight (FDA 2013).

The FDA claims responsibility for oversight of apps that allow patients to self-manage a disease or condition even if no associated treatment from a professional transpires. Patients may use the information for tracking and organizing the information regarding their current health status. These apps also make it easy for patients to view and use information. The document may be used for self-use or communicated to someone providing care for their conditions. The usage may create automated transfer and documentation of data, which might be stored in the patient's personal health record or the provider's electronic medical record (FDA 2013).

The FDA makes its regulatory decisions based on the intended use of a device. Many of the wearable devices contain sensors and the decisions regarding their regulation are based on the type of software used with the device and its usage. As for medical apps, the FDA does not regulate informational or educational devices; it does regulate diagnostic devices, meaning that a glucometer used by diabetics only displays the result. The software measures the blood sugar and is regulated (Baum 2014g).

The federal Medicare program has steadily expanded coverage of telemedicine services. About 20 states require private insurers to cover remote consultations the same way they cover in-person services (Landro 2014).

CMS updates for 2015 include coverage of telehealth services, which include annual wellness visits for the first visit and the follow-up visits with the caveat that such services also provide a personalized prevention plan (Conn 2014b).

Unique Device Identification System

The unique device identification system (UDIS) makes it possible to track devices used for patient care along with those used for monitoring care. The identification number tracking provides a way to monitor devices after they are approved for use (called *postmarket research*). The number is used for any recalls that are required for faulty or malfunctioning devices, which improves patient safety. The number can be documented in the patient's electronic record for future use.

Many medical manufacturers provide products to the international market creating a need for streamlining labeling for use in the global marketplace. Through the use of standardized identification, data pools and synchronization can occur.

Healthcare providers depend upon manufacturers to implement these numbers during the manufacturing phase; however, the providers still share responsibility for keeping track of the numbers. Besides the patient safety aspect of UDIS, the number is also useful in inventory management.

In addition to the FDA, the Federal Trade Commission (FTC) also shares responsibility for privacy issues. The FTC authorized a small study regarding data collection in fitness apps. The researchers found that once these health and fitness apps collected the personal data, the apps share it with third parties. Another study showed that each app works with 76 third-party collectors who provide information to companies for advertising and marketing. During this study, researchers found that 18 of the apps collected the unique device identifier or UDID along with the media access control (MAC) address (which controls the media address). Potentially, the data from various devices could be collected for a more complete picture of the individual (Sullivan 2014c).

The FDA maintains a global unique device identification database of all devices used in the United States. They also provide guidance to the industry about how to meet the standards related to UDIS. All devices are classified into three categories along with the associated time line for compliance. Labeling of packages for Class III devices was required in 2014, Classes I and II in 2015, and the remaining Class II in 2016. Direct marking on devices is due in 2016 for Class III products, in 2018 for Class II products, and 2020 for Class I products (FDA 2013). Many departments including regulatory affairs, quality assurance, supply chain, information technology, graphics/label design, packaging, engineering, customer service, brand protection and marketing, commercial trade, sales and operations planning, and master data management will be affected by these unique device identification (UDI) rules.

In his testimony before the Department of Health and Human Services, Dr. Joshua Rising testified that including the UDI in insurance claims would improve postmarket surveillance of FDA-approved devices. It would also create one central location for finding implanted devices. The EHR documentation is inconsistent and hard to find due to the lack of interoperability between electronic medical record systems (Saxena 2014c).

FDA Rules for Drug and Device Advertising

The FDA has published guidelines for drug and device advertising that require the inclusion of the risks associated with the product. The information must be truthful and not misleading. Consumers need to know what they are buying and what to expect from the performance along with any risks that might occur during usage. The FDA looks for a balance between the risk and benefit information. In addition, the benefits and risks must be prominently displayed so the consumer does not need to search for the risks. Since Twitter has 140 character limitations, the tweet can contain a link to additional information. The FDA will monitor the material on the landing page included in the tweet to determine if it meets the requirements (FDA 2014).

Regulating Fitness Apps

The Federal Trade Commission (FTC) has studied fitness apps (2014) to determine what data they capture and how it might affect the privacy of the individual who uses the app. These apps collect and transmit data about the body and the user. The researchers found that of the 76 companies, 18 of them captured the unique device identifier (UDID) meaning that they know the address of the device holding the app along with the International Mobile Station Equipment Identity (IMEI). If an app on the device collects exercise information and diet information, it is possible to link this information. Currently, there are no regulations for privacy concerning this sensitive information (Sullivan 2014c).

Too Much Reliance on Technology

As much as technology improves access, diagnostics, and quality of care, one caveat exists. If the physician fails to perform a physical examination by hand, there are some signs that can be missed and are only evident by listening to the sounds of the body and feeling the organs and lymph nodes. Sometimes, the use of technology guides the physician in the wrong direction, which a physical exam would avoid. Some medical schools such as Stanford and Johns Hopkins focus on the need for physical exams and include it as part of their training (Boodman 2014).

Ensuring the Safety of Data

In addition, many of the electronic medical record software products contain the cut and paste function. This shortcut often creates inaccurate entries. The entry is not edited for changes and erroneous data remains in the chart. For instance, a physician may remove a drain, but the copy and paste function may contain a description of the drain and the drainage for the previous shift when in fact there was no drain and no drainage, which makes for a conflicting and inaccurate update. For this reason, the American Health Information Management Association (AHIMA) has gone on record to eliminate this function.

The only way to secure the transfer of data from one entity to another is to use encryption; however, most software vendors do not include this function; and when it is added onto their product, they claim it invalidates their security features; therefore, most organizations shy away from the risk of adding encryption.

Verizon analyzed 63,000 security episodes and approximately 1,300 breaches from 50 data-sharing partners. Verizon discovered that most data breaches (46%) occurred from either loss of unencrypted devices or physical theft of the device. The researchers found that most organizations fail to encrypt mobile devices and laptops. The healthcare employees were negligent in the way they secure these devices in their personal homes and personal automobiles. Even with the lapse of security, encryption would protect the data (McCann 2014b).

Apple and IBM teamed up to partner in the development of secure apps for use in healthcare and insurance contained in the product, IBM MobileFirst platform. IBM's background in security solutions for their hardware will bode well for the partnership with Apple. Their security strategy includes IBM's cloud storage capability (Lopes 2014; Sullivan 2014). In addition, IBM will supply enterprise solutions that come preloaded on iPads and iPhones. IBM concentrates on big data, analytics, mobile device management, and security.

Privacy and Surveillance

Predictive analytics combines data from several sources in order to link it to create a complete picture. The University of Pittsburgh Medical Center combines patient claims, census records, medical records, and prescriptions to create a medical picture of the patient. It also combines consumer data from Axiom that provides education, income, marital status, race, household income, ages of persons in the household, and ownership of autos and homes. The combined data creates a way to segment high-risk populations and to provide more resources to them; however, it also creates concern that it could create an unequitable provision of medical care or a more tiered system. For instance, researchers found that Internet shoppers and those who use mail orders were the most likely to use the emergency department (Singer 2014). Through the use of predictive analytics in combination from multiple data sources, the most costly patients can be determined and interventions can be created to change their behavior. People in the United States pride themselves on a culture of autonomy and free agency. Yet, another concern revolves around the use of private information (Figure 3.1).

The HIPAA law requires privacy and confidential measures for patients' personal and private information; however, much of the data used to study populations is not covered under the law. Data derived from Google, medical-related

Figure 3.1   FDA to regulate apps that record health data. (From Sullivan, M., *VentureBeat*, May 16, 2014, http://venturebeat.com.)

social networks, healthcare product purchases online or through credit cards, sharing preferences by liking a product, sharing locations, or purchasing a product detrimental to an individual's health can all be acquired and tracked, often right down to the individual. The Federal Trade Commission possesses responsibility for individual rights in this area. They released a report stating that data brokers retain 3,000 pieces of data on every consumer in the nation (McCann 2014f).

Licensure

In order to ensure safe, quality care for patients, the department of health in each state regulates license requirements for all healthcare professionals. With the advent of telehealth and telemedicine, the need for licensure in multiple states results. For this reason, the Federation of State Medical Boards drafted legislation for states to expedite licensing requirements in multiple states. The compact is voluntary for both individual physicians and for states. Each state will still regulate practice; however, a physician in good standing in one state can achieve an expedited license in other states. This new compact allows specialists to provide services in underserved areas in another state, which is especially critical for patients with complex or rare diseases. To ensure the quality of care, the state medical boards will share information about issues and problems of individual physicians (Federation of State Medical Boards 2014a).

Conclusion

As innovation continues to develop, it can benefit individuals. The government's role is to ensure that the innovation does provide benefits and does not create any harm to the patient. Legislation creates rules for medical devices, new drugs, and monitors the use of nonmedical devices as they encroach into the medical realm.

In this age of apps and electronic records, an individual's private health information is readily available to hackers. Legitimate use of data for research requires a delicate balance between privacy and surveillance. Researchers need de-identified data; however, much of the data is still identified and could potentially create harm to individuals if the wrong people have access.

As technology changes the way healthcare is delivered, the state licensure boards also need to change. Licensure can come about through reciprocity. Each state board could maintain control and share information across state lines making it possible for providers to practice across state lines.

Discussion Questions

1. How are organizations overcoming the *top regulatory challenges* of telemedicine programs?
2. What impact has telemedicine had on *quality metrics*, including patient satisfaction?
3. mHealth creates more data. How much is too much when it comes to data and how should that information be safeguarded to prevent costly security breaches or HIPAA violations?
4. What happens when mHealth devices are not inter-operable with either one another or network infrastructures?

Assignment

Research innovations in technology as it relates to regulating new technology. Assess whether current legislation provides protection without restricting innovation. Identify issues related to regulation. Formulate solutions to identified issues.

Chapter 4

Intervention and Diagnostic Technology

Biosensing wearable or digestible devices provide data about the daily activities of individuals. Wearable forms include headbands, wristbands, watches and other jewelry, and smart clothing that detect vital signs and changes in physiologic signs (known as *biometrics*), including mood. The low cost of Bluetooth technology makes exchanging information from the biosensor to the smartphone app a low-energy exchange.

While the insurance industry and providers demonstrate an interest in the use of biosensors, individual consumers also show an increasing interest; however, most new users are the ones who are already fit. Patients show more interest after diagnosis of a problem than they do about using these devices for prevention; yet, as they spend more of their own money on insurance to cover healthcare diagnosis and intervention, their interest may increase. In that case, their interest will depend upon ease of use and meaningful feedback from the devices.

Wearables

Wearable biosensors come in many different shapes, sizes, and uses. A wearable headband called the *Muse* contains six sensors that detect brain waves and can locate brain waves that control critical thought, speech, and listening (Figure 4.1). The device can be worn throughout the day and rests on the ears. The device can pinpoint how different medications work on different areas of the brain. It can also be used to help patients identify stress and provide identification about when the patient could use stress-reducing techniques and change behavior. The outcome may provide data on how sleep, exercise, and food affect a person's mood (Ferenstein 2014).

Another wearable device that uses brain waves is one which helps patients use a computer through the use of their own thought processes. By connecting their own thoughts to a computer, the computer can initiate communication and potentially activity through use of a robot. In these early

Figure 4.1 A biologically controlled device—the Muse headband. (Image Credit: Sean Ludwig/*VentureBeat*. From Koetsier, J., *VentureBeat*, August 15, 2013, http://venturebeat.com.)

stages, the device can control the television, medical alert, and other simple devices; however, researchers hope to eventually link it to assistive devices to help quadriplegics and patients suffering from degenerative disorders such as Lou Gehrig's disease. Philips and Accenture jointly developed the Muse headband, which interacts and integrates technology using voice or eye commands. Users can preset messages for requests and voice commands (Millard 2014a).

Implantable defibrillators can transmit data right into the patient's chart. The data is analyzed and then inserted into the patient's private health record, which is also accessible by the patient. The patient information is recorded in an understandable format to keep the patients informed about their own health status. The data is also transmitted to the electronic medical record (Millard 2014a).

As the healthcare industry moves toward population health and value-based purchasing, there may be more interest on the part of patients and consumers in collaborating on their care and prevention of disease. Alignment between the consumer and the provider requires a partnership in improving their health status. Providers possess an interest in patient engagement that includes management of chronic disease, medication adherence, remote monitoring, and health promotion. People just want to feel good, optimize their daily functions, and ward off aging and disease. Population health and value-based purchasing will create a return on investment for treatment and prevention by using these devices and the care connected to them. These innovations will continue to improve; however, the real test is whether they will change behavior and truly make a difference in the health of the patients they serve.

3D and 4D Printing

At other times, the body needs external repair through surgery and other interventions. The use of 3D printing in manufacturing facilitates the creation of three-dimensional products, which medical device companies also use to build new body parts. The 3D and 4D printing advantage comes from this ability to create the parts without the need for traditional tooling that was previously necessary. Instead of injection molding, the production comes from placing several layers of product over and over again on the model. In healthcare, scientists project the ability to make replacement body parts from scaffolding and human tissue through 3D printing. Hearing aids and replacement joints are the most common medical manufacturing.

The technology includes scaffolding for building organs, joints, and tissue, and medical devices that often support existing human tissue. The scientific work targets the building of new tissue, organs, bones, and vessels. The ability to customize the body part makes 3D and 4D printing valuable and a wave of the future. Dentists can make a cap or implant for a tooth while the patient waits. Scientists have made livers that can be used to test new drug therapies and hope at some point to create and implant 3D manufactured livers in lieu of cadaver or living human transplants. Scientists have also created 3D brains for use by medical students, interns, and residents as part of their training (Doyle 2014) (Figure 4.2).

Figure 4.2   A 3D printing of an ear. (From Phillips, S., *Inside 3DP*, September 4, 2014, http://www.inside3dp.com.)

These 3D printing devices can take images from MRIs and make models from these images. It helps in diagnosis and treatment plans. Often, the new model shows defects that were not seen on the diagnostic image. The creation of these models makes it easier to teach interns and residents about physiology in the body and to design parts for use in learning how to perform a surgery. The process starts with MRI or CT images, which are used to create the plan for the body part providing the opportunity to build personalized, specific prostheses to repair defects caused by birth defects, trauma, or disease (Knight 2014).

Children with scoliosis often receive a prescription for a bulky uncomfortable back brace. Due to the discomfort, they do not wear it as long or as often as they should. 3D print-ing can create a custom-fitted device that is comfortable, trendy, and easy to wear. The 3D Systems Bespoke back brace looks so good that nonpatients want one. It is lightweight and breathable and looks more like a girdle made of a mesh pat-tern. Since the brace is fashionable, comfortable, and easy to wear, children comply with their treatment plan (Ruhe 2014c) (Figure 4.3).

One of the most costly, hard to diagnose, and hard to treat conditions involves the lower back. A new device containing sensors can analyze and transmit the analysis to a physician showing back motion and identifying problem areas. The four sensors include a magnetometer, gyroscope, and accelerator along with diagnostic electromyography sensors. These sensors provide information used to create specific treatment plans for patients. Insurers estimate that over $200 million is spent on unnecessary back fusions and other back surgeries that occur every year (Saxena 2014a) (Figure 4.4).

Another innovation for back surgery includes a 3D expand-able, interbody cage called *FLXfit*, which allows for bone growth within the cage. The implant surgery is performed through the scope for a minimally invasive approach that reduces recovery time. Previous spinal fusion technology

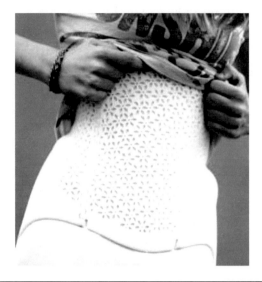

Figure 4.3 The 3D Systems Bespoke back brace (www.3dsystems. com) can be used to treat scoliosis. (From Ruhe, N., *MedCity News*, June 19, 2014, http://medcitynews.com.)

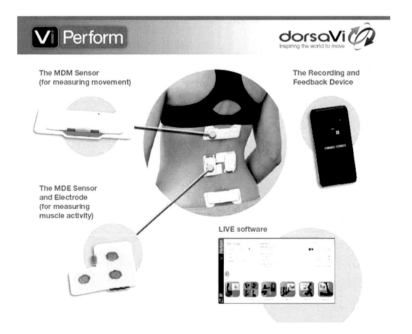

Figure 4.4 Back sensor devices. (From ViPerform, 2014, DorsaVie, Plymouth, MN, http://www.dorsavi.com/us/sport/viperform/.)

required open surgery; the implant was inflexible and patients often complained about the pain from the hardware. Many patients eventually returned to surgery to have the hardware removed (Saxena 2014b).

In addition, a whole new field of bioengineering is transpiring. So much so that three universities in Europe partnered with Queensland University of Technology in Brisbane, Australia, which initiated a master's program in bioprinting, the technique of using 3D printers to grow human tissue. These research centers also recognized that they could cut administrative supply costs. Open source 3D printing technology can provide a consumer savings in the range of $300 to $2,000 a year by printing 20 products annually (Byers 2014).

Rest Devices saved more than $250,000 in a year after purchasing a 3D printer, which cost $2,000. Rest Devices bought the printer to assist in rapid prototyping for research and development. The company began to develop sensors for an adult shirt that logs an individual's respiration, temperature, and body position, and the data to diagnose sleep apnea. The researchers evolved the original idea into a new use for infant monitors. Using 3D printers for more than hundreds of sensor prototypes, Rest Devices was able to save on production costs (Byers 2014).

The use of 3D printing evolved into 4D printing. This evolution involves the ability of tissues to sense changes in the environment and react to them, and in some instances, the cells can assemble themselves creating bioprinting, artificial tissues, smart sensors, and artificial organs. The company, ViaCyte, is working on the development of an artificial pancreas developed from stem cells inside of a retrievable and immune-protective encapsulated medical device. After implantation of the beta cells, they mature into endocrine cells that can secrete insulin and other hormones just as an original pancreas. This innovation may cure type 1 and type 2 diabetic conditions and relieve these patients from the need for insulin dependence and injections (ViaCyte 2014) (Figure 4.5).

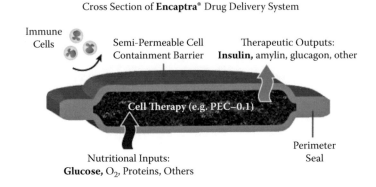

Cross Section of **Encaptra®** Drug Delivery System

Immune Cells

Semi-Permeable Cell Containment Barrier

Therapeutic Outputs: **Insulin,** amylin, glucagon, other

Cell Therapy (e.g. PEC–0.1)

Perimeter Seal

Nutritional Inputs: **Glucose,** O_2, Proteins, Others

Figure 4.5   Cross section of the Encaptra Drug Delivery System. (From ViaCyte, 2014, San Diego, CA, http://viacyte.com/products/vc-01-diabetes-therapy/.)

Prosthetics

In addition to 3D printing, customization in prosthetics and orthopedic appliances creates another opportunity for innovation. Since prostheses are often uncomfortable, new products are necessary. The prosthetic often chafes the skin creating pressure sores; however, a new product adapts to the body as a responsive and augmentative artifact. This product can adapt to the body over time in terms of materials, response, geometry, and design. Since it can take on any shape, its uses include inserts and sockets that adjust to the changes that occur within the body every day as part of normal fluctuations. The more malleable and adaptable the material, the less likely it will compromise skin integrity (Alexander 2014) (Figure 4.6).

A new device attached to the wrist, Supernumerary Robotic Fingers, adds two extra digits to the human hand. One located near the thumb and the other next to the fifth finger provides the wearer with more dexterity. It contains interlinking sensors that exert the same amount of pressure that human fingers do when grasping something. The device was designed for people suffering from arthritis; however, it may assist surgeons in delicate operations where hand fatigue occurs (Keenan 2014).

Figure 4.6 A durable prosthetic leg. (From Eveleth, R., *NovaNext*, March 5, 2014, http://www.pbs.org/wgbh/nova/next/tech/durable-prostheses/.)

Better than prosthetics, the ability to regenerate body parts creates more mobility and less stress on the body. Tissue Regenerative Systems created a reabsorbable implant for large missing bone segments due to orthopedic oncology procedures or trauma. Another product is a bioresorbable, reconstruction skeletal implant to fix burr holes made for skull surgery. The technological advantage is that no metal screws are necessary to secure it in place. The innovators see many more uses for this technology (Baum 2014d) (Figure 4.7).

Researchers at the University of Utah developed a 3D microscopic needle capable of providing images that are 70 times smaller than the width of a human hair. The quality compares to expensive microscopes. The needle can be implanted into the brain for imaging the function at the cellular level (U of U Press Release 2014).

Big Company Interest

The big companies, Google, Microsoft, and Apple, have all started to investigate the health market as a new strategy to grow their businesses.

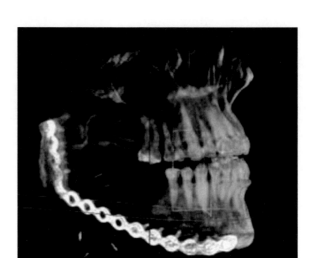

Figure 4.7 Reconstruction of a jaw. (From Tissue Regeneration Systems, 2014, Plymouth, MN, http://tissuesys.com/product-and-market-opportunities.)

Apple announced a $1.5 billion investment in a partnership with EPIC software and the Mayo Clinic. They plan to integrate wearable, fitness, and health devices into medical records to provide the physician with a more accurate picture of a patient's fitness, health, and potential problems. Apple calls this app *HealthKit*. HealthKit provides another opportunity to engage patients, encouraging them to monitor and comply with their treatment plans to keep their bodies healthy and in balance. Much like patients who monitor their blood pressure and blood sugar, the new apps can monitor other parameters for discussion and intervention by providers (Carr 2014) (Figure 4.8).

In 2008, Google ventured into the fitness industry with Google Fit when it was announced in January 2013 with a new release of the device planned for 2015. The device was designed to aggregate data from wearable fitness applications. The apps measure steps taken, heart rate, and inserts into Google's cloud-based services. The Android product dominated 80% of the smartphone market in 2014 and the new Google Fit could increase their market share (Olson 2014) (Figure 4.9).

Figure 4.8 Apple health app (Apple HealthKit). (From Carr, D., *InformationWeek,* **June 3, 2014, http://www.informationweek.com.)**

Google's partnership with AbbVie points to a new focus on drug research for diseases with cures or good treatment options such as neurogenerative diseases like Parkinson's and muscular dystrophy. Google can fund the project and through the investment generate new income (Barr and Loftus 2014).

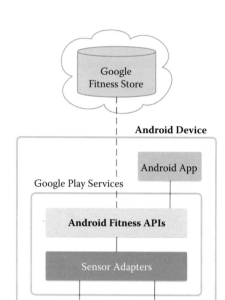

Figure 4.9   Google Fit on the Android. (From Android APIs, Google Developers, 2014, https://developers.google.com/fit/android/.)

Health plans partner with technology to try to meet the meaningful use requirement that patients have access to their own medical records and that they understand what the records mean. As an example, Aetna created a personalized health data platform called *CarePass*. They ran it for 1 year and announced in August of 2014 that they were discontinuing their exploration in this realm noting they learned from the experience, but it did not meet the goals identified for its use to improve patient access to their own data, tracking activity, and test results (Comstock 2014b) (Figure 4.10).

Researchers studied health and fitness apps on 6,800 iPhones and iPads and found that the use of these apps grew 87% faster than the total mobile industry during the first half

Figure 4.10   CarePass Daily Activity Tracker. (From Comstock, J., August 20, 2014b, *Mobihealth News*, http://mobihealthnews.com.)

of 2014. Consumer purchases of these apps showed a 62% increase over this 6-month period (Goedert 2014a).

In addition, 27% of 5,000 broadband users routinely access a fitness device connected to exercise equipment and an app on their smartphone. Another 13% stated they planned to buy equipment that interfaces with a fitness app during the upcoming year (Parks Associates 2014).

Decision Support

Radiologists review the referral reason, the patient's history, and any other pertinent information about the patient as part of their analysis of diagnostic images. They use computer-assisted reading to ensure they do not miss anything. New technology can also guide them to abnormal images that might not catch their attention. Computers possess artificial intelligence and use adaptive learning to continually improve what they do and to augment human capabilities (Kim 2013).

Sometimes, physicians just want to consult with one another. A group of physicians started an online forum named *Medting*. The cloud-based platform creates an opportunity for secure login where physicians can post test results, charts, and ask for advice or bounce their diagnosis off one another. Both the patient and the physicians are anonymous ensuring privacy and confidentiality for all involved (Quinn 2014).

Conclusion

As scientists develop more ways to monitor the body, individuals can proceed with their normal daily activities confident that providers can keep them healthy by sharing physiologic information directly to their providers. This sharing of data ensures early interventions that inhibit disastrous and untoward effects of their diseases.

At the same time, scientists are learning how to print body parts and create prostheses that work like the natural body. They also devise assistive devices that augment the function the patient has. Through the use of data, the accuracy of diagnosis and treatment improves through the use of programming that provides decision support information.

Discussion Questions

1. Identify innovative wearable devices and discuss their usage. Include the pros and cons of using these wearable products.
2. The advent of 3D and 4D printing makes it possible to create new body parts. What advances and issues are present in the current literature?
3. Can the use of decision support curtail critical thinking and impede patient care? Can provider autonomy and decision support coexist?

Assignment

Investigate new developments in regenerating body parts. Describe the difficulties encountered and how scientists have overcome them. Discuss the ethical issues. Compare transplant versus regeneration issues.

Chapter 5

Social Media Use in Health

Social media plays an important role in marketing for most businesses. The main difference in social media marketing is the feedback received from the customer. It provides a forum for listening not available from other media. The biggest mistake that companies make is to set their social media up and never revisit, improve, or monitor it. LinkedIn and Twitter are the two most commonly used outlets. Analytic software can identify links from social media to the company's Web site, which provides data on how effectively the social media environment targets interested patients.

Patients use social media to find information about their health status, disease, and diagnosis. Some insurers, hospitals, and health systems create their own Facebook site or other form of social media in order to engage patients, provide information, and add value. The asynchronous capability of social media allows people to engage on their own time schedule. The number of people interacting with one another is limitless.

Growth in social media has increased due to usage patterns in all age groups including the elderly. More people read the news online as opposed to the traditional newspaper;

therefore, many healthcare organizations have added social media to their marketing and outreach efforts. They can educate patients with information specific to treatments and diseases while marketing treatment options. The anonymity of posting on social media provides another reason why people like this type of interaction. Yet, individuals can receive support and motivation through the social media group. Two sites, CarePages (https://www.carepages.com) and CaringBridge (http://www.caringbridge.org) allow users to provide updates on their own health status and communicate with others with the same diagnosis. Privacy settings allow users to restrict who sees their postings. The individual posting the information also finds this format easier since communication can occur to a large group of friends and family with just one posting.

Cleveland Clinic surpassed 1 million users to its social media content in June of 2014. Leadership at the Cleveland Clinic determined that to engage patients and to create loyalty, they needed to provide knowledge to their constituents in a friendly and informative way. Primarily, they use Facebook as their platform for disseminating this information. Their digital engagement team collaborates with colleagues from different areas of the organization, who create ideas for the blog and provide the best expert sources. On their site, they publish a calendar known as *HealthHub* that contains and distributes information across the social channels in ways that maximize appeal to their respective audiences. Interestingly enough, the posting schedule and preferred techniques are different by channel; however, the strategy is fundamentally the same: use of HealthHub content makes a positive difference in people's health (Aiello 2014).

Cleveland Clinic posts six times a day on Facebook, which is more than most of their competitors. Tests show that this schedule works as evidenced by the engagement numbers. The goal is to strike a balance between wellness and prevention and clinical treatment information. The team constantly reviews the data to determine appropriate blog topics and combinations of words, images, videos, and graphics to create engaging posts on each social platform. Cleveland Clinic uses Facebook, Twitter, and YouTube to disseminate this information (Aiello 2014).

Covered California uses Facebook, Twitter, Google+, and YouTube as part of its health insurance exchange information and patient education. The state healthcare exchanges found that younger consumers prefer social media and are more likely to learn about offerings through this medium. Social media also works in remote areas where face-to-face meetings are not possible (Selvam 2013).

As baby boomers age, they need more healthcare and more education about how to stay healthy. They are the least likely to use the computer to find information; however, this trend is changing as organizations provide more information to engage this generation. For instance, Live Long Health (Livelonghealth.com) provides them with health information and resources along with support, relevant news, discussion groups, and posts times and places for screening services, which will help them age in an optimum state of health. Live Long Health partnered with Alliance Health Networks to provide this service (Brimmer 2012).

Students in the computer science department at the University of Rochester in New York developed a tool that scans tweets about food poisoning. They use GPS information embedded into the tweets to determine where the poisoning occurred. By using these GPS coordinates, the software provides a 97% accurate identification of the restaurant location. The team evaluated 3.8 million tweets over 4 months that were traced to 23,000 restaurants and involved 480 likely food poisoning cases. They monitor the GPS location for 72 hours after the first posting (Thomas 2013).

The other use for social media involves monitoring postings of patients to determine mood or deterioration in mental health status. For instance, the Navy-Marine Corp Relief

Society asks marines to use Facebook and to friend a staff member. (The staff members possess a professional account separate from their personal account.) Most patients join and then forget about it; however, the staff members monitor what these patients post and when concerned, they send a text message or initiate a phone call to perform further assessment. The use of social media for teaching and monitoring enhances the patient engagement to optimize the relationship and provide advice, teaching, and interventions (Neuhauser 2014).

Researchers at Perelman School of Medicine found that only 14% of health policy researchers used Twitter (645 million users) and about 20% used Facebook or blogs to communicate their research findings. The rationale for lack of use centers on the perception that academia views these sources as less credible, filled with opinion rather than facts, and therefore, deem published, peer-reviewed journal articles as more credible. Yet, younger researchers viewed the use of social media as useful and in a more positive light (Grande 2014).

Pharmaceutical companies need to monitor usage and reactions on drugs. They use social media to scour the postings for relevant content about their drugs. They monitor both sales and reactions. The Tufts Center for the Study of Drug Development researched how 12 pharmaceutical companies use social media as part of their clinical research. Of these companies, 75% do not formally gather information on adverse events connected to their drugs; however, they do monitor adverse events posted on social media. Treato, an Israeli social media company, monitors 1 million conversations a day that are posted on Facebook and WebMD. Through these postings, they can often determine the reasons why patients switch drugs (Iskowitz 2014).

Nearly 77 million people in the United States do not understand medical terminology and this low literacy rate affects their compliance with treatment plans resulting in readmission to the hospital and untoward complications. Social media can use infographics to demonstrate meaning and improve patient comprehension (Theilst 2012).

The U.S. Department of Health and Human Services (HHS) provides guidelines* for using social media. The leaders at HHS use social media to provide information and to collect information. During the swine flu epidemic, HHS used social media to provide information about vaccinations, other information, and also to dispel rumors containing inaccurate information.

Based on all these uses of social media, researchers reviewed Facebook pages to determine the applicability of its content. They found only about 9.5% of Facebook pages contained patient information specific to chronic diseases, while patients look to them for specific information. The majority of the pages (32%) were specifically designed for marketing. The research findings also identified that almost 21% of Facebook pages dedicated to disease seek to raise awareness and another 15.5% offer information that can be found on Wikipedia (Verel 2014b).

Invasion of Privacy

Insurance companies, providers, and employers can all track an individual's activities and locations while wearing medical devices. They can test productivity, how often an employee collaborates with others, and so on. While Gownder (2013) touts this ability as a way to improve productivity and customer satisfaction, individuals, however, worry about their privacy. The ability for the payor, provider, and employer to possess this much data on an individual creates some privacy concerns.

People sign up for data storage on devices like Fitbit from Apple and SAMI from Samsung. Currently, the data storage occurs in individual silos meaning that it is private and never aggregated for any kind of study. Now that Samsung (SAMI) and Apple (HealthKit) rolled out their healthcare platforms,

---

* Social Media at U.S. Health and Human Services (http://www.hhs.gov/web/socialmedia/).

people will want to study it for trends. The privacy question will arise as to who owns the data. Do these companies own the data that can be used for public health planning or does the individual own and control it (Sullivan 2014b)?

Social media accounts like Facebook and Twitter can cause damage later in life as people mature, look for new jobs, or do not want their children to see some of their previous actions. New companies such as Social Sweepster will scan and clean these accounts by removing inappropriate photos and words. Now that it is easier to post things in the moment, people regret these postings later and want them removed (Roston 2014). In addition, the European Union ordered Google to allow individuals to erase information that the individual deems harmful. Those opposed to the ruling state that individuals could remove important information that could alert victims to potential danger from another individual (Robinson, Schechner, and Mizroch 2014).

Discussion Questions

1. Can social media improve the health status of the population?
2. Does monitoring social media use by patients infringe on privacy rights?
3. Describe the benefits to society of monitoring social media.
4. How does the government use monitored social media?

Assignment

Research current uses of social media for health information or monitoring. Prepare a short article alerting patients about how their postings are monitored and what they can do to protect their own privacy.

Chapter 6

Healthcare Reform and Risk Management in Technology

Patient privacy protection was enacted as law in 1996 with the Health Insurance Portability and Accountability Act, known as *HIPAA*; however, over the last decade, few physicians fully complied with the law. Of physicians, 70% note they do little to regulate mobile devices as part of their protection of private, patient information. In addition, 31% of the 1,400 surveyed reported that upon implementation, employees receive few rules about how they can use their own devices at work and what security precautions they should take. The easiest method to secure these devices is to install a password and only use encrypted data. Surprisingly, only 61% reported that they back up the data they have. Most providers (69%) have never conducted a risk assessment to determine the vulnerability of their data (Westgate 2014).

As more and more people depend on apps for healthcare, the risks escalate. For instance, malicious codes can fool users into thinking they are authentic. Two credit unions identified a rogue app in January 2010 that tricked users into sending private financial information to cybercriminals. When identified, it was found that this same hacker had written 50 other malicious codes. The only way to secure apps is to ensure the use of code signing certificates. Third-party issuers ensure that malicious coders do not self-sign the certificates (Ganapati 2010).

Another way to isolate personal apps and files from company files comes from the use of sandbox technology. It was first developed as a way to isolate untested code from tested code; however, new usage has isolated personal files and apps from infecting company apps and files by limiting crossover of potential malware.

Chief Information Security Officer

The biggest challenge that chief information security officers (CISOs) face includes balancing protection of private health information (PHI) in compliance with HIPAA and ensuring that everyone who needs access to the PHI can access it. HIPAA rules and requirements increased with the latest revisions, which provided the need for organizations to implement the role of CISOs. In addition, the introduction of mobile technology created the need for tighter controls, access, and the ability to wipe the data off a mobile device in the event of a potential or actual threat.

In addition to mobile technology, medical devices such as infusion pumps and imaging equipment can also pose a threat. These devices can all push data to the Internet where hackers can pick up the data and use it maliciously (Gregg 2014b).

The CISO needs to itemize all of the different types of IT content managed in the organization and the associated security requirements. Access should be determined by need with limits on access to limit exposure to confidential content. Educate employees on their roles, access, and the security measures they need to employ to keep the PHI secure.

Experts agree that the healthcare industry is the least prepared for cyber attacks, and threats continue to increase. The Identity Theft Resource Center stated that 353 breaches occurred by midyear 2014 with more than half of them in healthcare. In addition, these criminal advances have doubled since the year 2000 (Pittman 2014).

Medical Identity Fraud

The Health Information Technology for Economic and Clinical Health (HITECH) Act required that healthcare providers convert from paper to electronic records by the end of 2014. In addition, the Patient Protection and Affordable Care Act required that electronic medical records contain two elements, intercoperability and meaningful use. Interoperability means that users can read the information contained in electronic medical records regardless of the vendor.

Meaningful use contains certain parameter requirements by year. For instance, initially, all records were required to contain vital signs, computerized physician orders, and electronic prescribing. Each year additional requirements are required. The adoption of electronic records does provide an opportunity for medical identity fraud and inappropriate access and use of private, confidential health information of individuals. Some think that the first-level criteria was enough and that Stages 2 and 3 are unnecessary. Their rationale is that it takes about 3 years to develop, install, fix problems, change workflow, and ensure competency of the users.

Beginning with the HIPAA requirements for breach notification, 1,000 breaches have occurred involving 500 individuals, which were reported to Health and Human Services (HHS). These breaches potentially affected 32 million people. In addition, HHS obtained 95,000 complaints. From these reports and investigations, they levied greater than $25.1 million in fines against these organizations. The Ponemon Institute reported that the total cost of breaches has reached $5.6 billion annually (McCann 2014f).

Hackers or insiders can access patient information that allows them to seek medical care and have it billed to another's insurance company. Auditors have instituted tools that run in the background to detect fraud. One factor involves the identification of significant height and weight changes. At Kaiser, the auditors look for natural progression like prenatal and postnatal care or newborn and infant care, where there is no record of the birth (Caramenico 2014).

As electronic records continue to increase due to federal mandates, rates of medical identity theft will increase. In 2013, there was a 19% increase in victims meaning that 1.8 million people suffered medical identity fraud (Antonio 2014c). Fraudulent use can also occur from within an organization. Employees can sell the information they access. For instance, an emergency room registrar in Florida sold 12,000 names to attorneys who used the information to pursue accident cases. The average victim loses $22,000 due to the theft (Antonio 2014c).

News regarding medical identity theft affects trust between patients and providers. In 2014, the Harvard School of Public Health asked patients about their concerns. Of the 1,500 respondents, 12% stated they withheld sensitive information from providers due to security concerns about their private information. Extrapolation of this 12% means that nationally, 38.2 million people withhold critical information from their providers (McCann 2014c).

The Department of Justice reported that the Medicare Fraud Strike Force filed 137 cases and 234 of 345 people charged pled guilty to fraud charges. These cases provide $8 in return for every $1 spent on fighting fraud (Antonio 2014c).

An easy way to mitigate fraud originating from an employee is to institute the level of access, meaning that employees can only access the information they need to perform their duties. Monitoring usage identifies unusual access patterns, requiring a more detailed and focused audit. Use encryption to secure transmitted data. Screening software can review every outgoing e-mail for characteristics that identifies disclosure of protected health information. Use an outside vendor to perform a security audit (Antonio 2014c). The audit should include everything the organization does to secure data from the technical, administrative realm, and from a physical standpoint.

Encryption on every device protects the data from both internal and external attacks. Encryption is especially critical for tablet usage. The devices also require a setup that allows for remote removal of all data if the device is lost or stolen. Storing patient information in the cloud rather than on devices is another way to keep the data both private and secure. The 2014 Verizon Data Breach Investigation Report concluded from 63,000 security episodes that 1,300 breaches (46%) came from physical theft of a device or unencrypted data (Verizon 2014).

In Stage 3 of meaningful use, patients need access to self-management tools to take responsibility and engage in their own care as one element for improving the health of the population. The patient portals provided by many healthcare systems, private physicians, and pharmacies fit within this criteria. The downside is that they are not connected.

Reimbursement Fraud

The federal government mandate for implementation of elec-tronic medical records improves patient care by ensuring that every provider who treats a patient has all of the past medical history including diagnosis and treatment. This avail-ability ensures safety by avoiding duplicate tests, prescribing known drug–drug interactions, and known allergies to drugs. At the same time, Health and Human Services paid physicians $22.5 billion in incentives to adopt electronic records; this change makes it easier to duplicate for fraudulent billing.

In order to mitigate fraud, providers need to check for cloned records and to audit for reliability of the data. Some medical record software allows providers to update notes to existing records or to create new records where there were none in the past. With this knowledge, other software manufacturers include a self-check audit; however, many buyers never use the function (O'Donnell 2014).

Do No Harm

The Hippocratic Oath contains the phrase, "Do no harm." Many times, the intervention for disease causes harm to the patient. There is more focus on not doing any harm during treatment. Diagnostic imaging tests provide good information for diagnosis; however, exposure to radiation occurs with every test. New capabilities make it possible to use the most appropriate test with the least amount of radiation tailored to the individual patient. For instance, dense breast tissue requires different imaging than nondense breasts. The choices include 3D images, ultrasound, MRI, and PET scans, each with its own capabilities, advantages, and drawbacks. It is also possible to reduce the grids to minimize radiation exposure in pediatrics and small adults (Rodriguez 2014).

Telemedicine Regulation and Usage

Telemedicine provides access to specialists in rural areas and primary care access for some rural residents. All 50 states regulate telemedicine differently as to how it can occur, who can participate, and policies and procedures required. The American Telemedicine Association decided to try to make sense out of the disparity. They used 13 indicators to rate each state. The majority of the states earned a "C" grade for use of telemedicine (Figure 6.1).

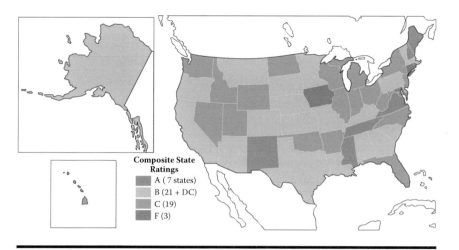

Figure 6.1   Ratings by "grade" for the regulation of telemedicine in the 50 states. (From the American Telemedicine Association, 2014.)

As new laws develop, improved access to healthcare results through the use of telemedicine. Even in states with high grades for telemedicine usage, the practitioners are not aware of the changes in laws and regulations. Laws in some states limit telemedicine growth. Florida, Idaho, and Montana ranked the worst for physicians. The five worst states for regulating Medicaid telemedicine usage are Utah, Connecticut, Idaho, Hawaii, Rhode Island, and West Virginia (Thomas and Capistrant 2014).

Discussion Questions

1. As the U.S. healthcare system moves forward with the Patient Protection and Affordable Care Act implementation, are there risks involved in individual privacy? Will personal health information be used to limit or allocate scarce resources and services? What can be done to preserve patient choice and autonomy?
2. The Medicare program suffers from fraudulent billing, which the government has never been able to control. As a larger share of medical payments depend on the government as the payor, will fraud proliferate? How can fraudulent billing be contained and mitigated?

Assignment

Research current government billing fraud. Determine the cause of the fraud. Propose a plan to deter fraudulent billing and to catch those who engage in fraud.

Chapter 7

Healthcare Analytics Use in Population Health

In the business world, leaders use the terms *big data* and *business intelligence*. Healthcare analytics or healthcare informatics are actually terms for the same thing. Data collection and aggregation provide an opportunity to look for patterns and based on these patterns to make decisions to improve quality and decrease costs. The driver of this change comes from the payment shift from volume to value inherent in the Patient Protection and Affordable Care Act (PPACA). It augments the Health Information Technology for Economic and Clinical Health (HITECH) Act, which requires the implementation of electronic medical records (EMRs).

A 2014 survey of the most wired health systems shows that data in isolation means nothing. In fact, 36% of hospitals share their information with community health record exchanges ensuring a more complete picture of a patient's medical history. Another 71% of the most wired providers actively managed care transitions from acute to long-term care or home care compared to 57% of the total respondents. Health systems (43%) also find that clinical and claims data together create a way to stratify the population and prioritize needs in order to create a more healthy population. In addition, 69% retrospectively analyze the data for quality improvement and cost reduction (Millard and McCann 2014).

As technology continues to improve and all types of care include computer documentation that interface through mobile medical applications, patients can review, revise, and provide input into their electronic record for both individual use and for improving the health of the population. The improved, real-time communication through the use of patient portals and real-time documentation from medical sensors allows for improved research results increasing the accuracy of focused data capture. Real-world evidence creates new opportunities for evidence-based treatment regimens. Increased data sharing also provides a database for retrospective and predictive analytics.

A good example of using these tools in clinical trial research involves the use of a calculator to determine cardiac risk in patients with rheumatoid arthritis. Thirteen centers in 10 nations use this tool to predict the development of cardiac problems over a 10-year period. No single center had enough data to create a meaningful database for the study. The ability to aggregate the data from all 13 centers created the opportunity for a credible and significant study (Goth 2014c).

Drug manufacturers create narrow studies to determine the efficacy of their drugs during the premarket phase. In the postmarket phase, they want to look at other factors that might be changed when using the drug. For this reason, Merck has initiated a trial using 20,000 patient sites in several countries to test the impact of a diabetes drug. Merck wants to study what happens in the everyday life of a patient taking its drug, Januvia. This study will include multifaced data contained in electronic medical records, combined with patient generated questionnaires. The study will evaluate incidents of hypoglycemia, blood sugar control, and quality of life to obtain a more complete picture of use and reactions to the medication (Meek 2014).

Revenue Cycle Management

The confluence of regulation for EMRs and payment reform creates the need for good data to be used for both clinical applications and for improving the business of healthcare. Revenue cycle management is one area for improvement, which means automating coding and billing, and avoiding claims rejections. This means starting the cycle when patient scheduling occurs. At every step of the patient encounter, employees need to check and double check the accuracy of the data input. Automation of claims ensures quicker payments, but only if the claims are clean, accurate, and free from other errors. According to The Electronic Payments Association (NACHA 2014), more than 8 million healthcare claims were automated using the national clearinghouse in January 2014, which was the first month that required health plan compliance with the newly adopted healthcare electronic fund transfer standard transaction. The sum of these transactions was approximately $45 billion in payments from health plans to providers.

In addition, good data provides information about what the patient owes upfront. This knowledge means that collecting the patient's portion of the bill can begin more quickly. Historically, providers waited until after the insurer paid their portion of the claim. The contract information that includes the patient's portion of the bill is readily available upon admission. At that time, patients can provide a check or charge card. The payment of the patient's portion of the bill upfront reduced accounts receivable days and the potential for bad debt. If the patient cannot meet the obligation, a payment plan or charity option can also begin at that time, which reduces stress on the patient and family and improves the revenue cycle.

Many payors also include patient satisfaction as part of the contract. The creation of a stress-free and seamless experience for patients increases satisfaction. Most patients want to know upfront what they will owe. A patient-friendly process can begin during scheduling and registration and can prevent surprises and a negative experience later. Typically, the revenue cycle steps begin with the first patient encounter and may also be the last interaction. Therefore, a good process free from surprises results in a positive experience. Good data shared between physician offices and hospital departments creates a collaborative partnership that reduces denials and increases reimbursement.

Data for Improvement

Data comes from charting patient complaints, diagnoses, test results, and treatment plans. From this information, acuity and outcome assessment identifies criteria for change. One focus of improvement revolves around the need to streamline work processes. Nurses at Florida Hospital Celebration Health agreed to wear a GPS-like device that tracks their movements. The nurses were promised that the tracking would only be used for improvement purposes. For 3 years, the data was used to create efficient changes in care that satisfied both the nurses and their patients. One analysis showed that just as many nurses were needed for the patients at night as are needed during the day (Pecci 2014a).

The best decisions based on data require a full set of data from the disparate information systems used in the organizations. Disparate data requires normalization, standardization, and for unstructured data, it requires structuring. Only about 20% of the data in the EMR is structured.

The data stored in the EMR can be used to predict events and outcomes. After analyzing patterns, valid predictions about when a patient needs intervention can result. These predictions offer the opportunity to prevent an untoward event. Prevention saves money. For instance, the United States spends $55 million annually on missed predictions; spends $210 billion on unnecessary care; and spends $130 million on inefficient care (Optum 2014). Analytics identifies who receives the most care from organizations and what care is the most costly. This identification makes it possible to use predictive analytics on these areas to both improve the quality and reduce the cost of the care. Nationally, the three most costly care conditions include diabetes, chronic obstructive pulmonary disease (COPD), and congestive heart failure (CHF). Identification of these three populations and the use of evidence-based medicine can ensure the financial viability of the organization, especially with the new focus on paying for population health instead of treatments.

In many cases, analysis of test results occurs through computer algorithms before they are even sent to the physicians. Groups of lab values are analyzed together along with imaging results, which create more accurate diagnoses. These algorithms successfully interpret electrocardiograms and are often as accurate as human experts; yet, the combination of artificial intelligence and human validation creates even more accuracy and decreases errors of omission. Imaging software can direct attention to suspicious areas. In addition, the results from the tests can create alerts for intervention before the patient seeks emergency care (Topol 2014a).

Another use for data comes from a cooperative agreement between Washington state emergency physicians, the Washington State Hospital Association, and payors who created a statewide database, which captures the name, data, and reason for a patient's visit to an emergency room (ER). This way, physicians know the recent history of any patient who has visited an ER. It decreases costs to the state Medicaid budget and increases the quality of the care that the patient receives by identifying abuse or a need for more intensive treatment (Weise 2014).

Population Health

A good starting point in understanding patient population involves the aggregation and analysis of data that identifies the economics and demographics of the population served, along with their preference for the sites they use to obtain care, and finally the types of care they seek. Next, the most costly and most common care is analyzed in order to initiate treatment and prevention plans. Analysis of these treatment and prevention plans must occur continuously in order to understand what works and what does not work.

Wearable and implantable devices ensure that the at-risk segments of the population with expensive chronic conditions are monitored and that early intervention occurs, which maintains these patients' optimal level of health status. An example of an implantable device is the congestive heart failure device, which monitors pulmonary artery pressure and heart rate. Patients with class III heart failure often experience multiple hospital admissions in a year. The monitor alerts providers of the need to adjust therapy, improve function, and reduce the need for hospitalization (Slabodkin 2014a).

The more information a provider possesses about the patients they serve, the more they can make a difference in the health of the population. As the paradigm shifts from episodic care to coordinated longitudinal care (population health), systems need to be developed that ensures providers receive test results and act upon the data. When a patient is hospitalized, they routinely receive care from a hospitalist who orders tests. These patients may be discharged before all of the results are received. Historically, the primary care physician had no knowledge about these pending test results. Brigham and Women's Hospital in conjunction with Partners in Health designed an automated system that sends these pending test results to the primary care physician. The outcome of their research was a 76% increase in response to the results versus a 38% response in a control group (Dalal et al. 2014).

Dictation Translated to Text and Coding

One of the requirements for population health involves maintaining accurate records. Legislation has required the adoption of Electronic Health Records (EHRs) and standardized coding for billing using ICD-10 codes. At the same time that reimbursement continues to decline, clinicians are turning to technology to increase their productivity. One new development involves the use of computerized medical dictionaries that translate words or phrases into the required computer language known as *SNOMED CT*. The guidelines for certifying EHR products now requires the use of SNOMED codes (Conn 2014a).

Research

Registry trials allow for large-scale research that saves money and creates an opportunity to easily enroll patients and to collect data in a low-cost way. These clinical registries provide a standardized methodology for collecting demographic and quality data. Registry trials can aggregate the results of trials more quickly than the traditional randomized trials that were so costly. The retrospective outcome of data currently requires an extra step in data entry. The next phase will include exporting data automatically from the EMR.

Discussion Questions

1. Describe the use of big data to improve processes, decrease costs, and increase the quality of care.
2. The focus on revenue cycle management has developed due to the changes in payment contained in the Patient Protection and Affordable Care Act. Describe how organization leaders are addressing revenue cycle management.

Assignment

Describe the use of big data by providers, payors, and the government. Describe how their usage differs. Identify areas where they can collaborate and areas where they should remain separate. Analyze whether or not the use of big data has improved the health of the population.

Chapter 8

The Future

Using the Body to Cure Itself
and Realigning the Body for Health

A common theme for healthy bodies espouses the need for
exercise. First, physicians prescribe exercise to increase the
heart rate. An increased heart rate increases perfusion and
studies show that it actually changes some of the components
in the blood. For instance, chronic inflammation occurs in
patients who do not exercise. For some reason, the debris that
collects in the body deposits without exercise.

Chronic inflammation causes heart disease, arthritis,
Crohn's disease, and a myriad of other diseases including
hypertension, asthma, diabetes, infertility, and obesity.
Researchers discovered that electronic shock (bioelectronics)
to nerves can decrease the inflammatory response in the
body. They have found that the use of electric shock in the
right doses can create the same response as expensive drugs
in reducing the inflammatory response (without the side
effects from drugs). Vagus nerve stimulus mitigates production

of the tumor necrosis factor, thereby reducing inflammation. Stimulus to the vagus nerve creates a body-wide response to mitigate inflammation (Behar 2014).

Another promising treatment, called *optogenetics*, involves the integration of optics and genetics to manipulate opsins (natural proteins) to turn off and on certain neurons in the body. Optogenetics can target specific cells in the body creating a local response rather than a system-wide response (Yizhar et al. 2014).

The body can often repair itself with just a little help. A new technique for repairing rotator cuff tears of the shoulder does just that. The old technique used staples to attach the tissue to the bone; however, the staples often pulled through the tissue destroying the repair. The new technique uses bovine tissue to create a scaffold that allows blood products to bind and build around it to create a strong repair comprised of new tendon tissue (Lobo 2014).

Another way the body heals itself occurs when all the good bacteria create a medium for healing. This means ensuring that the bad elements are identified and modified as needed. For example, a test strip used to identify bad bacteria early on creates an opportunity for early intervention. The test strip identifies elevated protease activity, which indicates wound healing (90%) and graft failure. The bacterial strips identify the bacteria long before they show up in any other kinds of tests (Keshavan 2014a).

EpiBone uses the body's own stem cells to create replacement bone for loss of bone from trauma, cancer, or a genetic defect. An anatomically precise pattern is made to correct the patient's defect. Then, the patient's own stem cells grow into a framework that creates a perfect fit. The graft requires one surgery instead of multiple surgeries, which are often required for other methods. Since the patient's own stem cells create the bone graft, no rejection occurs (Keshavan 2014b).

A fusion device also allows a patient's tissue to integrate with an implanted device. The device includes a series of roughened topographies at several levels: macro, micro, and cellular. The osteogenic property of the device creates more stability and long-term function since the natural bone morphogenic protein can grow in the surface environment of the implant (Dyrda 2014).

After an injury, patients receive physical therapy; however, new research states that simple exercises to realign the body and build muscles around joints can actually prevent injury and arthritis caused by excess weight and malalignment. In other words, as part of prevention, people need preventative physical therapy. One such program comes from MobilityWOD, which provides techniques and tools for creating good body alignment. It occurs through basic exercise that one performs for maintenance (MobilityWOD 2014) (Figure 8.1).

In addition, researchers found that walking 12,000 steps a day can reduce the effects of ingesting fructose. A sedentary lifestyle forces the pancreas to work harder to metabolize glucose. The combination of limiting sugar and exercising every day can ensure that the pancreas works properly and can help stave off diabetes (Mullarky 2014).

Figure 8.1   Exercise can be used to realign the body. (From MobilityWOD, 2014,   http://www.mobilitywod.com/dailyrx/#.)

Natural Healing

Scientists have discovered that a healthy gut includes beneficial microbes. This discovery spawned a new food category using probiotics to create the healthy flora in the bowel. Within the population, 20% suffer from irritable bowel syndrome and other problems associated with the bowel (Williams 2010). Patients can take a probiotic as a supplement or in yogurt to create the natural element necessary to properly function and digest food.

Nutrition scientists continue to study how diet affects the body. Research in two studies presented to the European League Against Rheumatism (EULAR 2014) found a direct relationship between monounsaturated fatty acid and increased disease states in rheumatoid and osteoarthritis patients (Scientific Blogging 2014).

In addition, people with chronic diarrhea can receive treatment in the form of fecal transplant material from a relative who has healthy flora. These patients often suffer from clostridium difficile as the predominant bacteria in the bowel. The healthy bacteria are absent due to an imbalance in the medium. Causes include a genetic predisposition to irritable bowel syndrome or the overuse of antibiotics. The infusion of the fecal material corrects the problem as the new bacteria grows and builds the natural flora needed (Van Nood et al. 2013).

Creating an internal healthy environment has led researchers to explore skin conditions. Their findings have also confirmed the need for a balance of healthy flora on the skin. AOBiome is a mist developed for the skin that contains healthy bacteria and fungi that create the perfect balance. Therefore, AOBiome treats both oily and dry flaky skin conditions and acne problems. Interestingly enough, the balanced mist also helps the skin fight off harmful bacteria like MRSA (AOBiome 2014).

The body also contains natural killer cells known as monoclonal antibodies. Researchers found that they could take these natural cells from the body of a pediatric leukemia patient and grow them outside of the body. "Researchers can design and produce antibodies, called monoclonal antibodies (mAb), that specifically target a certain protein like the ones found on cancer cells. In a previous paper, Heisterkamp showed that a mAb targeted to a specific receptor (BAFF-R) on the leukemia cells stimulated the Natural Killer cells to attack and kill the cancer. The BAFF-R mAb was also used in this study" (Children's Hospital Los Angeles Saban Research Institute 2014, p. 1). Once grown outside the body, they were able to reimplant them and they targeted the cancer cells. The reason the patient's own cells were used is because the body might reject donor cells and think they also are a threat. The research shows promise for treating patients after chemotherapy to ensure that all the cancer cells are destroyed (Children's Hospital Los Angeles Saban Research Institute 2014).

Scientists have used game theory to identify the life cycle of tumor cells. They have studied the mutation rates in conjunction with glucose and lactate levels to determine when tumors switch between different energy levels. Their hypothesis is that when changes in glucose and lactate levels occur, the metastasis of the tumor also occurs. If their hypothesis proves true, they could develop strategies to interrupt the life cycle (Goth 2014f).

Google Glass

Five years ago, no one could imagine Google Glass; however, healthcare providers started implementing its use in 2014. Google Glass provides information in a monitor format on the eyeglasses worn by the user. Since physicians spend one-third of the time (with a patient) searching for data on the computer, Google Glass expedites the process by providing the data in a corner of the eyeglasses. Applications move the data between the electronic health record and the eyeglasses (Lee 2013).

New apps, Drchrono, Augmedix, and Pristine, use Google Glass to directly add content to the patient's medical record. Physicians can record a procedure, add consultation notes, or other pertinent content using voice commands. Physicians see Google Glass as a wearable computer, easy to use, and which allows their hands to be free to do other things. Drchrono claims to have 60,000 physician users at mid-2014 and they are still growing (Farr 2014). Dignity Health physicians use Google Glass to increase the amount of time they spend on the patient versus the amount of time they spend looking at charts. Since users can ask Google Glass to find reports, they do not have to spend time entering and searching the computer database; instead of keying in their request, it becomes a spoken command. These physicians were able to reduce information search time, thereby transferring the saved time to actual patient care. These physicians averaged 15 to 20 patient visits per day; however, their efficiency increased as they previously spent 70% of their time on the computer and subsequently reduced it to 35% after implementing Google Glass, which allowed for more time spent with the patient. The doctors also reduced the time spent entering their patient notes from 33% preuse of Google Glass to 9% after implementation. They use the Augmedix app along with the Google Glass products (Boulton 2014a).

Physicians in the United States often provide training for physicians in developing countries. Through the use of Google Glass, physicians in the United States can see live streaming of what the surgeon sees and can provide real-time guidance to improve their practice during surgery. UCLA physicians connect with these remotely located surgeons and coach them, providing guidance as they perform surgery (Goth 2014f).

Emergency physicians stream live images of patient lesions to dermatologists to obtain consults in real time. They stream it live to protect the patient from pirates who might want to post inappropriate images on YouTube (AFP RelaxNews 2014).

Beth Israel emergency department physicians found a different use. They were able to connect Google Glass to their electronic tracking board. They could scan a code in the patient's room, which would immediately bring up the pertinent data about the patient and the reason for the emergency department visit. The eyeglasses were programmed for use with finger taps and voice commands for easy physician usage (Halamka 2014).

Video Glasses

In addition to Google Glass, dentists and interventional radiologists use video glasses as a way to distract anxious patients. They found that when patients became immersed in a video, they would block out their surroundings, which reduced their anxiety level. Those who experienced the most relief were women and patients who were the most anxious prior to the procedure (Netburn 2014).

Concierge Care

As healthcare plans become more expensive to the patient with less reimbursement to the physician, both parties look for a way to continue their relationship that provides value to both. One way is to combine concierge care with mHealth. Ringadoc acts as an intermediary, which collects all of the patient and payor information before connecting the patient and the physician. Then when they connect, they can both focus on the patient's problem. The telehealth capability helps the patient avoid costly deductibles for emergency room visits and at the same time maximizes the efficiency of the physician (Wicklund 2014f).

Genomics

Every living thing contains microorganisms including disease pathogens. In the past, it took years to analyze a small amount of DNA, but it now takes just seconds. Knowledge of the DNA makeup of a disease or a disease in a specific individual leads to individual treatment plans. After identifying DNA, researchers need to find the latest information and research specific to their identification. Now, they can use Watson, a computer, to comb through journals and research papers. The computer can search 23 million abstracts for review in just a few minutes.

While it is possible to conduct a full gene-sequencing test on individuals, it often provides useless results; however, in hard to diagnose cases, physicians can order specific exome sequencing tests that identify disease. Exome sequencing identifies DNA segments that code for proteins, exons. The patient's DNA is compared to a reference sequence for the human genome. Variants in the sequence focus on the disease, making diagnosis and treatment more efficient in diagnosing disease, mental retardation, cancer, cardiomyopathy, Lou Gehrig's disease, and epilepsy (MacDougall 2014).

Researchers target microbiomes to understand how they affect one's susceptibility to cardiovascular disease, obesity, and other chronic diseases. The goal behind this research is to learn how to manipulate the microbiomes to improve health much like probiotics are used today to create normal flora in the gut (F. Collins 2014).

A trial, funded by the National Institutes of Health, involved 20 people whose biopsies from glioblastomas and healthy tissues will be fed into Watson for analysis of mutations and possible treatments (Zimmer 2014). The outcome provides information on new drugs prepared specifically to attack genetic mutations that stimulate tumor growth.

Drug therapies for cancer traditionally focus on a recipe based on the diagnosis; however, new technology is based on smaller segments of the diagnosis population with the same genetic distinction. The advantages of these new, specific drugs are that they target the cancer cells without creating any collateral damage to the surrounding healthy tissue. In 2013, 80% of the newly approved drugs (50 drugs) by the FDA were for specific, target drugs (Brady 2014).

Historically, cancer tumors were treated based on tissue type; however, researchers have found that the type of cell matters more than the tissue. For instance, three types of breast cancer (HER2, luminal A, and luminal B) originate from different cell types. After analyzing 3,500 tumors that were found in 12 different tissue types, a comparison showed that cancer similarities occur based on the type of cell where the tumor originated rather than the type of tissue. This discovery means that the treatment needs to target the cell type rather than the tissue location. It also means changing tumor classifications based on cells rather than tissue type (Hoadley et al. 2014).

Memorial Sloan Kettering Cancer Center (MSKCC) also uses Watson. The center is highly ranked nationally for its cancer care. The difficulty in treating cancer is that cancer contains clusters of diseases and each of these clusters requires different treatment regimens. The treatment options continually change due to advances in science; therefore, physicians need assistance in finding the latest evidence-based treatments for their patients. Since MSKCC treats 30,000 cancer patients each year, Watson takes the information and matches it to specific patient information and published literature. Watson uses artificial intelligence; it can mine and identify specific treatments using cognitive computing (Bassett 2014).

WellPoint found another use for Watson's cognitive analytics. Insurance companies like WellPoint use case managers to make decisions about whether a patient is ready for discharge or needs more time in the hospital, making the patient care more effective and efficient. As the nurses input data about a patient's status, Watson analyzes the information and provides a recommendation with accuracy and confidence.

The next step is authorization of the treatment plan, which prior to automated real-time decision making took 72 hours (Ronanki and Steier 2014).

Bacteria continue to evolve and as they do, they develop resistance to antibiotics. For this reason, it is important for physicians to know the latest, most effective antibiotic for use with specific bacterial infections. Most physicians use a tool called *Epocrates* that provides this information. Physicians can access the app called *Epocrates Bugs+Drugs* for use as a decision support tool that identifies bacterial susceptibility by zip code. The app contains an algorithm that can sift through thousands of microbial data contained in a cloud. The data comes from all over the country, which is why the treatment decision depends on the patient's zip code (Meneghetti 2014).

Researchers have also created synthetic or artificial DNA that can be used to develop new kinds of vaccines, antibiotics, and other medical products. The artificial DNA was incorporated into bacteria. One safeguard built into the artificial DNA is that it requires an additive. If the additive is missing, the bacteria can no longer continue to reproduce. These findings produce a whole new field of treatment. The estimated size of biologic and protein-based therapies will be $165 billion by 2018 (Hotz 2014).

Another way to use nanoparticles to treat cancer is through the use of flecks of gold (particles). The nanoparticles are used in combination with radiation. They can be heated (hyperthermia) to damage cancer cells at the site of the tumor. They are also heated to liquefy fat for use in liposuction (Diep 2014).

People around the world suffer from diabetes. Researchers continually try to develop new medications and treatments to alleviate the damage from the disease. So far, no curative treatment has been derived; however, new research using gene technology shows promise. A researcher from Harvard developed a compound that inhibits the protein responsible for an insulin-degrading enzyme (IDE). It was developed using a DNA insulin-templated synthesis to identify how IDE inhibits the degrading of insulin that results in increased insulin levels in the blood. This research may contribute to a true cure for the disease (Rojann 2014).

Inherited blindness occurs through mutation of the gene RPE65 that causes a degenerative eye disorder. The Center for Cellular and Molecular Therapeutics uses a neutralized virus to transport a function gene to specific cells in the eye that cause the blindness in order to treat it (Pogoreic 2014c).

Scientists implanted a human gene that controls heart rate functions into pigs and it corrected the problem. As the research continues, they hope to eliminate the need for pacemakers since they require periodic maintenance and additional surgery (Naik 2014b).

In addition to using genomics to prevent the development of disorders, it is also possible to predict them. Scientists have constructed a formula that uses genotyping and phenotyping to identify DNA sequence alteration that manifests as an autism spectrum disorder (Uddin et al. 2014). This knowledge may provide a treatment in the future.

Iceland, Utah, and India contain homogeneity populations that were studied for DNA changes to discern why some groups of people are more likely to inherit a disease or have a susceptibility for certain diseases. Genetic mutations can cause specific cancers as well as birth defects (Goedert 2014b).

Researchers also discovered that the Amish population inherits a gene (APOC3) that keeps their bad cholesterol (LDL) low and keeps their hearts healthy. This population includes four mutations that destroy the function of this gene to keep the LDL at low levels. Those who inherit this mutation experience a 40% reduction in the triglyceride levels and a corresponding 40% decrease in risk for heart disease (Kolata 2014).

Another type of gene mutation, IL-10 receptor deficiency, creates irritable bowel disease (IBD). The immune cells do not regulate immune responses or create healthy immune cells. In children, the syndrome causes stunted growth in addition to anal abscesses and severe, bloody diarrhea. The most common treatment uses bone marrow transplants; however, the transfer of anti-inflammatory macrophages works just as well with less trauma and side effects (Fliesler 2014).

Nikon, facing a decreasing digital camera market, announced that it will pursue lithography technology for DNA chips used in genetic research. Other opportunities in healthcare are also under consideration similar to what Sony, Samsung, and Apple have done (Inagaiki 2014).

Mount Sinai Health System recruited a group of volunteers (30,000) for its Personalized Medicine Research, which combines the information in the EHR with a genomics platform called *CLIPMERGE* (Clinical Implementation of Personalized Medicine through Electronic Health Records and Genomics). These two databases work together to identify personalized treatment options. The researchers use clinical data representation combined with electronic phenotyping to create algorithms that automatically control status and assign cases for use in Genome Wide Association Studies. The outcome of this research is to expand the use of genomics for personalized medical treatment (Mace 2014d).

New technologies also make it possible to view single-molecule, cellular, and neurology processes through the use of a 3D super-resolution, flourscence microscopy. Scientists know a myriad of cell processes occur through single molecules. The 3D microscopy allows viewing of the structure of cells, their interaction, how they bind, and traffic (Vutara 2014).

Traditionally, new drugs are tested on a select population from Eastern Europe. Researchers have found differences in the efficacy of drugs between men and women. Genomics may determine the difference in the DNA of heart diseases like hyperlipids. Drug treatments that raise HDL, but do nothing to lower LDL, may be appropriate for one group of patients and not for another. The etiology of disease may differ between genetically different populations. The use of genetic data may lower the cost of bringing new drugs to market and also provide evidence of who will benefit from a drug treatment based on their genomes (Verel 2014b).

Immunotherapies

In addition to the DNA method of treating cancer, oncologists also use immunotherapy. T cells contain the ability to identify tumor growth and rush to the site of the tumor; however, in their present state, these T cells cannot kill the cancer cells. Scientists have discovered a way to increase the number of T cells to create a stronger attack on the tumor growth.

The T cells look for mutant proteins and when found, they trigger an immune antitumor response, which is called *adoptive cell therapy* (ACT). The therapy targets patient's cells (Tran et al. 2014). This therapy provides a more natural defense that avoids the adverse effects of chemotherapy.

Stem Cells

Stem cells provide the opportunity to generate new body parts and life saving components of blood and other body fluids. For instance, patients undergoing chemotherapy or suffering a hemorrhage from surgery or trauma need blood components. Platelet BioGenesis produces synthetic platelets starting with stem cells. They use a two-chamber method that mimics how the body produces platelets in the bone marrow. Right now, the company produces and supplies platelets to the blood supply inventory; however, as progress continues, labs may make their own onsite using the patient's own bone marrow cells (Pogoreic 2014b).

Some people are born without critical body parts. A female born without a vagina cannot have sex or deliver a baby. Yet, scientists are now able to grow a vagina and implant it into a patient. Vaginas both secrete mucus and can stretch and contract making them harder to develop. The new process starts by bathing a pig's intestine in detergent to remove cells from the tissue. Then, the patient's own cells biopsied from the genitalia and smooth muscle are inserted into the tissue.

One side of the structure is coated with the cells from the genitalia and the other with smooth muscle. Then, it is placed in a nourishing environment of an incubator until the structure grows sufficiently for implantation in the body (Naik 2014a).

Scientists also discovered that injecting a specific type of stem cell, mesenchymal, into the spinal cord of patients suffering from multiple sclerosis can reverse the disease. The stem cells decrease inflammation and provide a long-lasting result. The stem cells also regenerate the tissue surrounding the nerves. These stem cell injections also show promise in regenerating damaged cells in the brain (Weintraub 2014).

Minimally Invasive Procedures

Several years ago, the placement of cardiac stents surpassed open-heart surgery for repair of diseased (atherosclerosis) vessels in the heart and abdomen. The newest procedural change involves a nonsurgical heart valve replacement called *transcatheter aortic valve replacement* (TAVR). Patients need a valve replacement when the aorta narrows or the valve closes improperly, a condition affecting 1 million elderly patients (Johnson 2014).

Minimally invasive spine surgery decreases the time (30 minutes) needed to perform the surgery and also decreases the healing time. A good example is an implant, called *SpineJack*, developed for the treatment of vertebral compression factures. The implant realigns the spinal column by restoring the vertebrae to the original shape, which decreases pain and increases function. Physicians perform the procedure on an outpatient basis (Carmagnol 2014).

Employee Safety

One of the new realities in healthcare concerns the safety of the healthcare worker as patients demonstrate hostile behavior.

When confronting a dangerous situation, critical response support needs immediate attention. The use of badges connected to a central alert system allows the individual to call for help with the press of a button. Real-time locating systems (RTLS) identify where they came from and send an alert to tell the responders where to go (Penoza 2014).

Technology Adoption

Healthcare company leaders (27%) that adopt new technology early lead the market in both growth and revenue. More cautious leaders (27%) wait to see how technology performs. The most cautious (35%) wait until technology proves itself before adoption occurs (Harvard Business Reports 2014). A clear advantage transpires for the early adopters.

Microclinics

In competition with retail clinics, the newest entrant, called *microclinics*, operates without a human presence. Patients sit down in the Medex Spot cabin for assessment using stethoscopes, blood pressure cuffs, pulse oximeters, and otoscopes with more additions monthly. In addition, the cabin can clean itself between patients. The unmanned clinic does not exclude physicians, it provides diagnostics on low-level patients to determine if they do need to see a provider (Dunn 2014).

Radio Frequency Identification

The baby boomer generation took charge of their lives beginning in their teen years. They will probably do all they can to age in place. Radio frequency identification (RFID) is one way to help them find things they misplaced. When an RFID tag is placed on an item, it transmits a signal making it possible to locate lost items. Most systems provide a general location; however, Pixie can identify the location within inches. It is less costly and more accurate and relies on Bluetooth technology. Pixie works on a coin cell battery and has a reach of 150 feet (Clark 2014).

Conclusion

As medical advances continue, scientists learn more about how to use the body's natural properties to heal itself. The bacteria in the body known as *normal flora* keeps the body healthy. Diet and drugs affect this natural flora. As scientists discover more about how to keep the natural flora in balance, people enjoy an optimal health status. Rather than finding more drugs to fight the imbalance, scientists increasingly focus on using these natural properties.

As Obamacare implementation materializes, it creates more access to care for low-income individuals and decreases the care and coverage previously experienced by others. A two-tiered system is occurring for those who can afford more. Physicians who want to control their destiny and autonomy have created concierge care where they contract for cash payments instead of relying on the government or commercial payors.

Scientific advances in genomics and minimally invasive procedures comprise treatment interventions for patients that can decrease the recovery time. They also do less harm to the individual.

Discussion Questions

1. Investigate the use of Google Glass in healthcare. Evaluate the advantages and disadvantages.
2. Debate the issues concerning concierge care.

Assignment

Prepare an executive summary concerning the advancements in genomics and minimally invasive surgery. Compare the old method with the new method. Identify risks and advantages of the new methods. Assess costs and availability.

References

ABI Research. 2013. Wearable sports and fitness devices will hit 90 million shipments in 2017. *ABI Research*, February 22. Retrieved from https://www.abiresearch.com/press/wearable-sports-and-fitness-devices-will-hit-90-mi.

AFP RelaxNews. 2014. Google Glass being tested in dermatology consultations. *New York Daily News*, March 13. Retrieved from http://www.nydailynews.com/life-style/health/google-glass-tested-dermatology-consultations-article-1.1720256?print Page.

Aiello, M. 2014. Secret to Cleveland Clinic's social media success: Content. *HealthLeaders Media*, June 11. Retrieved from http://www.healthleadersmedia.com/print/MAR-305431/Secret-to-Cleveland-Clinics-Social-Media-Success-Content.

Alexander, L. 2014. Medical device design: Startup with dynamic material to make prosthetics fit better, quicker. *MedCity News*, June 19. Retrieved from http://medcitynews.com/2014/06/startup-interface-material-medical-device-design-make-prosthetic-fit-adjustable-quicker-comfortable/#ixzz35D6Mcxjx.

American Telemedicine Association. 2014. Washington, DC. Retrieved from http://www.americantelemed.org/.

American Well. 2014. Innovation in telehealth: Recording the doctor visit for future review. American Well. Retrieved from http://www.americanwell.com/howItWorks.html.

Andrews, J. 2014. Telehealth spurs big changes in care. *Healthcare IT News*, May 13. Retrieved from http://www.healthcareitnews.com/news/telehealth-spurs-big-changes-care?topic=17,29,26.

Annas, G. J. and Elias, S. 2014. 23andMe and the FDA. *The New England Journal of Medicine*, March 13. Retrieved from http://www.nejm.org/doi/full/10.1056/NEJMp1316367.

Antonio, J. 2014a. Controlling medical identity theft and fraud. Fierce Health Payer AntiFraud, May 12. Retrieved from http://www.fiercehealthpayer.com/antifraud/story/controlling-medical-identity-theft-and-fraud/2014-05-12.

Antonio, J. 2014b. To thwart ID theft, keep an eye on employees. Fierce Health Payer AntiFraud, April 6. Retrieved from http://www.fiercehealthpayer.com/antifraud/story/thwart-identity-theft-keep-eye-employees/2014-04-06.

Antonio, J. 2014c. Medicare fraud fighters deliver healthy ROI. Fierce Health Payer AntiFraud, January 29. Retrieved from http://www.fiercehealthpayer.com/story/medicare-fraud-fighters-deliver-healthy-roi/2014-01-29.

AOBiome. 2014. Pioneering bacterial therapy for skin. AOBiome. Retrieved from https://www.aobiome.com/company.

Arrigo, M. F. 2014. Easing the pain of prior authorization. *Healthcare Finance News*, July 9. Retrieved from http://www.healthcarefinancenews.com/blog/easing-pain-prior-authorization?single-page=true.

AuntMinnie. 2014. Mobile health market projected to surge. AuntMinnie. Retrieved from http://www.auntminnie.com/index.aspx?sec=sup&sub=ris&pag=dis&ItemID=106956.

Bailey, J. L. and Jensen, B. K. 2013. Telementoring using the Kinect and Microsoft Azue to save lives. *Int. J. Electronic Finance* 7(1). doi:10.1504/IJEF.2013.051755.

Baker, D. W., Brown, T., Buchanan, D. R., Weil, J., Balsley, K., Ranalli, L., Lee, J. Y., Cameron, K. A., Errreira, R., Stephens, Q., Goldman, S. N., Rademaker, A., and Wolf, S. 2014. Colorectal screening in a community health center. *JAMA Intern Med.* Published online June 16, 2014. doi:10.1001/jamainternmed.2014.2352.

Barr, A. 2014. Google's new moonshot project: The human body. *The Wall Street Journal*, July 27. Retrieved from http://online.wsj.com/articles/google-to-collect-data-to-define-healthy-human-1406246214.

Barr, A. and Loftus, P. 2014. Google, AbbVie announce research partnership. *The Wall Street Journal*, September 4. Retrieved from http://online.wsj.com/articles/google-abbvie-announce-research-partnership-1409764830.

Bassett, J. 2014. Memorial Sloan Kettering trains IBM Watson to help doctor make better cancer treatment choices. Memorial Sloan Kettering Cancer Center, April 11. Retrieved from http://www.mskcc.org/blog/msk-trains-ibm-watson-help-doctors-make-better-treatment-choices.

Baum, S. 2014a. Report: 19 million will use remote patient monitoring by 2018. *MedCity News*, June 26. Retrieved from http://medcitynews.com/2014/06/biggest-market-remote-patient-monitoring/#ixzz35rRMocNP.

Baum, S. 2014b. Entrepreneur hopes telemedicine + PT will stop pre-diabetes from becoming diabetes. *MedCity News*, June 13. Retrieved from http://medcitynews.com/2014/06/entrepreneur-hopes-telemedicine-pt-will-stop-pre-diabetes-from-becoming-diabetes/#ixzz34cstGgMZ.

Baum, S. 2014c. GE Healthcare app uses art and music therapy to stimulate minds of Alzheimer's disease patients. *MedCity News*, March 22. Retrieved from http://medcitynews.com/2014/03/ge-mind-app-hopes-stimulate-senior-minds-art-music/#ixzz2wnLXfAX9.

Baum, S. 2014d. J&J early stage collaborations span 3D printing for orthopedics, brown fat, biosensors. *MedCity News*, June 19. Retrieved from http://medcitynews.com/2014/06/jj-early-stage-collaborations-span-3d-printing-brown-fat/#ixzz35D9tki5u.

Baum, S. 2014e. Where digital health meets design. *MedCity News*, June 10. Retrieved from http://medcitynews.com/2014/06/apple-executives-chat-fda-wearables-medical-device-regulation/#ixzz34L6PhrsQ.

Baum, S. 2014f. Robotics milestone: FDA clears motorized exoskeleton to help paralyzed patients walk. *MedCity News*, June 27. Retrieved from http://medcitynews.com/2014/06/robotics-milestone-fda-clears-motorized-exoskeleton-help-lower-body-paralysis-patients-walk/#ixzz35sQQFIMC.

Baum, S. 2014g. Apple execs and FDA talk wearables and mobile device regulation nuances. *MedCity News*. Retrieved from http://medcitynews.com/2014/06/apple-executives-chat-fda-wearables-medical-device-regulation/.

Behar, M. 2014. Invasion of the body hackers. *The New York Times Magazine,* pp. 36–41.

Bennett, S. 2014. Google smart lenses get boost from Alcon owner Novartis. *Bloomberg News*, July 15. Retrieved from http://www.bloomberg.com/news/2014-07-15/novartis-allies-google-with-to-make-smart-contact-lens.html.

Bernard-Kuhn, L. 2014. The doctor will see you now—Virtually. *USA Today*, June 7. Retrieved from http://www.usatoday.

com/story/news/nation/2014/06/07/the-doctor-will-see-you-now—virtually/10171461/?utm_campaign=KHN%3A+First+Edition&utm_source=hs_email&utm_medium=email&utm_content=13123496&_hsenc=p2ANqtz-91BrtESr7TsezdHslJm-bvt EzXHGlMn0UMes9wzsV8Mopn_M31vV-wRXU8eVS7PZs0 dSNBf3sPJeKuQbxg9Eqy3YnRsLibNHxYEmqReicJCrd_-Fg4&_hsmi=13123496.

Bertolucci, J. 2014. TellSpec brings big data to dinner. *Information-Week*, April 4. Retrieved from http://www.informationweek.com/big-data/hardware-architectures/tellspec-brings-big-data-to-dinner/d/d-id/1174136?_mc=RSS_IWK_EDT&cid=NL_IWK_Daily_20140405&elq=%3Cspan+class%3Deloquaemail%3Erecipient id%3C%2Fspan%3E&elq=fe8718e61f834489ac2053d77cf8aa9c&elqCampaignId=1883.

Boodman, S. G. 2014. Technology displacing physical exams. *Healthcare IT News*, May 23. Retrieved from http://www.healthcareitnews.com/news/technology-displacing-physical-exams?single-page=true.

Bort, J. 2014. This company saved a lot of money by tracking their employees with Fitbits. *Business Insider*, July 7. Retrieved from http://www.businessinsider.com/company-saved-money-with-fitbits-2014-7#ixzz36zhLV7gU.

Boulton, C. 2014a. How Google Glass automates patient documentation for dignity health. *The Wall Street Journal*, June 16. Retrieved from http://blogs.wsj.com/cio/2014/06/16/how-google-glass-automates-patient-documentation-for-dignity-health/?KEYWORDS=health+reform&utm_campaign=KHN%3A+First+Edition&utm_source=hs_email&utm_medium=email&utm_content=13204694&_hsenc=p2ANqtz-9dsqUDZV96Wqd9dDrt0G 6CPEJJfc4DSSgY4hTnhergfGzJKvYSwZ4yvPbs_vDcWNorGIndZ SY18RuGnAfrCtXxm0mQMg&_hsmi=13204694.

Boulton, C. 2014b. Fitness tracking programs enter the big data challenge. *The Wall Street Journal*, June 24. Retrieved from http://blogs.wsj.com/cio/2014/06/24/fitness-tracking-programs-enter-the-big-data-challenge/tab/print/?KEYWORDS=health+insurance&utm_campaign=KHN%3A+First+Edition&utm_source=hs_email&utm_medium=email&utm_content=13289258&_hsenc=p2ANqtz—2EwzOaRjgWeEU4Pfs44qeW9y_y4DunOGwQ 7DJGvAQowsMjuSD6sj19tlavm-aWoYHVkeM7YAAiu1jNECL4VV tJoaF2g&_hsmi=13289258&cb=logged0.6282828117255121.

Bowman, D. 2014. VA telehealth efforts cut patient costs. Fierce Health IT, June 19. Retrieved from http://www.fiercehealthit. com/story/va-telehealth-efforts-cut-patient-costs/2014-06-19?utm_medium=nl&utm_source=internal.

Brady, D. 2014. Drugmakers find breakthroughs in medicine tailored to individuals' genetic makeups. *The Washington Post*, June 1. Retrieved from http://www.washingtonpost. com/national/health-science/2014/06/01/40127d1c-e107-11e3-8dcc-d6b7fede081a_story.html?utm_campaign=KHN%3A+Firs t+Edition&utm_source=hs_email&utm_medium=email&utm_ content=13053938&_hsenc=p2ANqtz—ieigY0U-rwn9hZ9pe FLoSaAYx8AYjqymABuKyJU8F9SgGmPM9zZIZy2ATP1r8d71 XVUZRftArSE0iTNRUKJRjC05Jd1ztKsiEMq90FukQ46-qPa8&_ hsmi=13053938.

Brandt, A. 2014. iPatient Care releases new patient centered apps. *Health Tech Zone*, July 23. Retrieved from http://www. healthtechzone.com/topics/healthcare/articles/2014/07/23/384524-ipatientcare-releases-new-patient-centered-apps.htm.

Brewster, S. 2014. MIT can now track a heartrate through a wall with Wi-Fi signals. *Gigaom Research*, June 13. Retrieved from http://gigaom.com/2014/06/13/mit-can-now-track-a-heart-rate-through-a-wall-with-wi-fi-signals/.

Brimmer, K. 2012. Social network aims to keep baby boomers healthy, prevent unnecessary costs. *Healthcare Finance News*, October 9. Retrieved from http://www.healthcarefinancenews. com/news/social-network-aims-keep-baby-boomers-healthy-prevent-unnecessary-costs?topic=05,19.

Brimmer, K. 2014. New technologies, hospital strategies promote patient engagement. *Healthcare Finance News*, June 2. Retrieved from http://www.healthcarefinancenews.com/ news/new-technologies-hospital-strategies-promote-patient-engagement?topic=,19,22.

Brunsman, B. 2014. Cincinnati Children's to help kids in Caribbean using telemedicine. *Cincinnati Business Courier*, July 1. Retrieved from http://www.bizjournals.com/cincinnati/ news/2014/07/01/cincinnati-childrens-to-help-kids-in-caribbean.html.

Byers, J. 2014. 3-D printing: Healthcare's new edge. *Healthcare IT News*. Retrieved from http://www.healthcareitnews.com/ news/3-d-printing-healthcares-new-edge?topic=10,28,19.

Caramenico, A. 2014. Medical ID theft: Red flags and opportunities. Fierce Health Payer AntiFraud, June 24. Retrieved from http://www.fiercehealthpayer.com/antifraud/story/medical-id-theft-red-flags-andopportunities/2014-06-24.

Carmagnol, C. 2014. VEXIM launches new generation SpineJack(R) device during SFCR Congress in Paris. *The Wall Street Journal*, June 9. Retrieved from http://online.wsj.com/article/PR-CO-20140609-906762.html.

Carnns, A. 2014. Health care apps offer patients an active role. *The New York Times*, April 26. Retrieved from http://www.nytimes.com/2014/04/26/your-money/health-care-apps-offer-patients-a-more-active-role.html?emc=edit_th_20140426&nl=todaysheadlines&nlid=7766146.

Carr, D. 2014. Apple partners with EPIC, Mayo Clinic for Health-Kit. *InformationWeek*, June 3. Retrieved from http://www.informationweek.com/healthcare/mobile-and-wireless/apple-partners-with-epic-mayo-clinic-for-healthkit/d/d-id/1269371.

CDC. 2014. New CDC data show declines in some diabetes-related complications among U.S. adults. Centers for Disease Control and Prevention, April 16. Retrieved from http://www.cdc.gov/media/releases/2014/p0416-diabetes-complications.html.

Children's Hospital Los Angeles Saban Research Institute. 2014. Natural killer cells battle pediatric leukemia. *ScienceDaily*, August 19. Retrieved August 23, 2014 from www.sciencedaily.com/releases/2014/08/140819082908.htm.

Chouffani, R. 2013a. mHealth clinical apps impacting care, not just with consumers. TechTarget. Retrieved from http://searchhealthit.techtarget.com/opinion/MHealth-clinical-apps-impacting-care-not-just-with-consumers?asrc=EM_ERU_27369471&utm_medium=EM&utm_source=ERU&utm_campaign=20140320_ERU%20Transmission%20for%20 03/20/2014%20(UserUniverse:%20732731)_myka-reports@techtarget.com&src=5223540.

Chouffani, R. 2013b. mHealth apps access hidden mobile data to improve patient care. TechTarget. Retrieved from http://searchhealthit.techtarget.com/opinion/MHealth-apps-access-hidden-mobile-data-to-improve-patient-care?src=5248389&asrc=EM_ERU_29606116&uid=16343684&utm_medium=EM&utm_source=ERU&utm_campaign=20140526_ERU+Transmission+for+05%2F26%2F2014+%28UserUniverse%3A+870707%29_myka-reports%40techtarget.com.

Clark, D. 2014. Can't find your keys? Just look at your phone. *The Wall Street Journal*, September 15. Retrieved from http://online. wsj.com/articles/cant-find-your-keys-just-look-at-your-phone-1410812551?tesla=y&mod=djemTEW_h&mg=reno64-wsj.

CMS. 2014. Telemedicine. Centers for Medicaid and Medicare Services. Retrieved from http://www.medicaid.gov/Medicaid-CHIP-Program-Information/By-Topics/Delivery-Systems/Telemedicine.html.

Collins, F. S. 2014. The future of medicine is about you. *The Wall Street Journal*, July 7. Retrieved from http://online.wsj.com/articles/francis-collins-says-medicine-in-the-future-will-be-tailored-to-your-genes-1404763139.

Collins, S. 2014. Pocket diagnosis. University of Cambridge, March 19. Retrieved from http://www.cam.ac.uk/research/news/pocket-diagnosis.

Combs, V. 2014. Diapers that analyze urine could reduce UTIs among people with dementia. *MedCity News*. Retrieved from http://medcitynews.com/2014/03/diapers-analyze-urine-reduce-utis-…ories&utm_medium = email&utm_term = 0_c05cce483a-cbf5ceae2c-67008541.

Comstock, J. 2013. Five reasons virtual doctor visits might be better than in-person ones. *Mobihealth News*, May 8. Retrieved from http://mobihealthnews.com/22215/five-reasons-virtual-doctor-visits-might-be-better-than-in-person-ones/.

Comstock, J. 2014a. PwC: Care delivery disruption will spur new health economy. *Mobihealth News*, April 14. Retrieved from http://mobihealthnews.com/32047/pwc-care-delivery-disruption-will-spur-new-health-economy/.

Comstock, J. 2014b. Exclusive: Aetna to shut down CarePass by the end of the year. *Mobihealth News*, August 20. Retrieved from http://mobihealthnews.com/35976/exclusive-aetna-to-shut-down-carepass-by-year-end/.

Conn, J. 2014a. IT experts push translator system to convert doc-speak into ICD-10 codes. *Modern Healthcare*, May 3. Retrieved from http://www.modernhealthcare.com/article/20140503/MAGAZINE/305039969/it-experts-push-translator-systems-to-convert-doc-speak-into-icd-10.

Conn, J. 2014b. Proposed CMS rule expands telehealth payments, domain. *Modern Healthcare*, July 7. Retrieved from http://www.modernhealthcare.com/article/20140707/

NEWS/307079945&utm_source=AltURL&utm_
medium=email&utm_campaign=mpdaily?AllowView=VXQ0Unp
wZTVEZlNaL1IzSkUvSHRlRU91ajBzZEErSlk=.

Cook, D. 2014. Fitness trackers work best with incentives. Benefits
Pro, April 24. Retrieved from http://www.benefitspro.com/
2014/04/24/fitness-trackers-work-best-with-incentives.

Coombs, B. 2014. Why your boss wants you to see online doctors.
CNBC, July 10. Retrieved from http://www.cnbc.com/
id/101823566.

Cox, J. 2013. Monitoring, app-enabled devices & cost savings
2013–2018. Juniper Research, July 17. Retrieved from http://
www.juniperresearch.com/reports/mobile_health_fitness.

Cue. 2014. Fierce Medical Devices. Retrieved from http://www.
fiercemedicaldevices.com/story/mobile-medical-app-brings-
laboratory-testing-home/2014-06-12.

Dalal, A. K., Roy, C. L., Poon, E. G., Williams, D. H., Nolido, N.,
Yoon, C., Budris, J., Gandhi, T., Bates, D. W., and Schnipper,
J. L. 2014. Impact of an automated email notification system
for results of tests pending at discharge: A cluster-randomized
controlled trial. *Jamia* 21(3). Retrieved from http://jamia.bmj.
com/content/21/3/473.full#ref-3.

Desjardin, D. 2014. Remote monitoring exploring new territories.
HealthLeaders Media, May 8. Retrieved from http://www.
healthleadersmedia.com/print/TEC-304292/Remote-Monitoring-
Exploring-New-Territories.

Diabetes News. 2014. Newly found widespread gut virus may be
connected to obesity and diabetes. *Diabetes News*, July 28.
Retrieved from http://www.diabetes.co.uk/news/2014/jul/
newly-found-widespread-gut-virus-may-be-connected-to-
obesity-and-diabetes-92008856.html.

Diana, A. 2014. Telehealth gains momentum in Obamacare era.
InformationWeek, April 17. Retrieved from http://www.
informationweek.com/healthcare/mobile-and-wireless/
telehealth-gains-momentum-in-obamacare-era/d/d-id/1204479.

Diep, F. 2014. Gold nanoparticles melt your excess fat. *Popular
Science*, June 18. Retrieved from http://www.popsci.com/
article/science/gold-nanoparticles-melt-your-excess-fat.

Dowskin, E. and Walker, J. 2014. Can data from your Fitbit trans-
form medicine? *The Wall Street Journal*, June 23. Retrieved
from http://online.wsj.com/articles/health-data-at-hand-with-
trackers-1403561237#printMode.

Doyle, K. 2014. 3 ways 3-D printing could revolutionize healthcare. Quartz. Retrieved from http://qz.com/139585/3-ways-3-d-printing-could-revolutionize-healthcare/.

Dunn, L. 2014. Are micro clinics the future of healthcare delivery? *Becker's Hospital Review*, September 15. Retrieved from http:/www.beckershospitalreview.com/leadership-management/are-micro-clinics-the-future-of-healthcare-delivery.html.

Dyrda, L. 2014. Titan spine gets Australia, New Zealand thumbs-up on endoskeleton fusion device. *Becker's Spine Review*, June 25. Retrieved from http://www.beckersspine.com/orthopedic-a-spine-device-a-implant-news/item/21321-titan-spine-gets-australia-new-zealand-thumbs-up-on-endoskeleton-fusion-device.

The Economist. 2014. The quantified self. *The Economist*, March 3. Retrieved from http://www.economist.com/node/21548493.

Emmi Solutions. 2014. Motivating people to take action: Improving population health with technology. Retrieved from emmisolutions.com.

Eustis, S. 2013. Telemedicine and M-health convergence—Markets reach $1.8 trillion by 2019. Convergence occurs as patients become more responsible for care delivery. WinterGreen Research. Retrieved from http://www.wintergreenresearch.com/reports/telemedicine%202013%20press%20release.

Eveleth, R. 2014. When state-of-the-art is second best. *NovaNext*, March 5. Retrieved from http://www.pbs.org/wgbh/nova/next/tech/durable-prostheses/.

Farr, J. 2014. Startup launches "first wearable health record" for Google Glass. *Reuters*, June 12. Retrieved from http://www.reuters.com/article/2014/06/12/us-google-health-idUSKBN0EN2MG20140612.

FDA. 2013. Unique device identification. U.S. Food and Drug Administration. Retrieved from http://www.fda.gov/MedicalDevices/DeviceRegulationandGuidance/UniqueDeviceIdentification/default.htm?utm_source=Members-Only+Updates&utm_campaign=c7c1e8c870-Proposed_Rules_7_5_2012&utm_medium=email.

FDA. 2014. Guidance for industry. Food and Drug Administration, June. Retrieved from http://www.fda.gov/downloads/Drugs/GuidanceComplianceRegulatoryInformation/Guidances/UCM401087.pdf.

Federation of State Medical Boards. 2014a. Understanding the medical licensure compact. Federation of State Medical Boards.

Retrieved from http://www.fsmb.org/state-medical-boards/
advocacy-policy/interstate-model-proposed-medical-lic.

Federation of State Medical Boards. 2014b. Model policy on the
appropriate use of telemedicine technologies in the practice of
medicine. Federation of State Medical Boards. Retrieved from
http://www.fsmb.org.

Ferenstein, G. 2014. Enough hype: Here's what Interaxon's brain
sensing headband (Muse) can do today. *MedCity News*, May.
Retrieved from http://medcitynews.com/2014/05/enough-
hype-heres-interaxons-brain-sensing-headband-muse-can-
today/#ixzz331Q8SwYQ.

Flaherty, J. 2014. A beautiful at-home medical device that cuts out
trips to the doctor. *Wired*, June 12. Retrieved from http://www.
wired.com/2014/06/a-beautiful-at-home-medical-device-that-
cuts-out-trips-to-the-doctor/#slide-id-960811.

Fliesler, N. 2014. Cell therapy for early-onset inflammatory bowel
disease? Mass Device, June 24. Retrieved from http://www.
massdevice.com/blogs/massdevice/cell-therapy-early-onset-
inflammatory-bowel-disease-0?page=show.

Fox, S. and Duggan, M. 2013. Health Online 2013. Pew Research
Internet Project, Pew Research Center, January 15. Retrieved
from http://pewinternet.org/Reports/2013/Health-online/
Summary-of-Findings.aspx.

Freedman, D. H. 2014. The trillion dollar cure. *INC.*, February.
pp. 94–108.

Ganapati, P. 2010. Malware sneaks into Android market. *Wired*,
January 14. Retrieved from http://www.wired.com/2010/01/
android-malware-fears/.

GeeksWorld. 2014. American Well® finds video is key to telehealth
diagnosis. *GeeksWorld*, February 5. Retrieved from http://www.
broadwayworld.com/bwwgeeks/article/American-Well-Finds-
Video-is-Key-to-Telehealth-Diagnosis-20140205#.Uy3AxNzBSpc.

Gleason, R. 2014. Telemedicine program aims to reduce waiting
times for psychiatric services. *Midland Reporter-Telegram*,
May 25. Retrieved from http://www.mrt.com/top_stories/
article_841fa4cc-e476-11e3-a3df-0019bb2963f4.
html#ixzz32x3jhCQg.

Goedert, J. 2014a. Can Google succeed with health apps?
Health Data Management, July. Retrieved from http://www.
healthdatamanagement.com/news/Can-Google-Succeed-with-
Health-Apps-48247-1.html.

Goedert, J. 2014b. Vendor offers isolated gene pools for analysis. *Health Data Management*, June. Retrieved from http://www.healthdatamanagement.com/news/Vendor-Offers-Isolated-Gene-Pools-for-Analysis-48200-1.html?utm_campaign=daily-jun%209%202014&utm_medium=email&utm_source=newsletter&ET=healthdatamanagement%3Ae2723900%3A3722191a%3A&st=email.

Goldberg, S. 2014. Telemedicine gains ground in treatment of injured workers. *Modern Healthcare*, July 7. Retrieved from http://www.modernhealthcare.com/article/20140707/INFO/307079989?AllowView=VDl3UXk1TytDdk9CbXgzS0M0M3hlMFNwaUVVVZEF1OD0=&utm_source=link-20140707-INFO-307079989&utm_medium=email&utm_campaign=dose&utm_name=top.

Google Research. 2012. The digital journey to wellness: Google/Compete Hospital Study. Google/Compete. Retrieved from http://ssl.gstatic.com/think/docs/the-digital-journey-to-wellness-hospital-selection_research-studies.pdf.

Gorman, A. 2014. No time to see the doctor? Try a virtual visit. *Kaiser Health News*, September 16. Retrieved from http://capsules.kaiserhealthnews.org/index.php/2014/09/no-time-to-see-the-doctor-try-a-virtual-visit/.

Goth, G. 2014a. Telemedicine proves accurate for preemie eye screening. *Health Data Management*, July. Retrieved from http://www.healthdatamanagement.com/news/telemedicine-proves-accurate-for-preemie-eye-screening-48361-1.html?utm_campaign=daily-jul%205%202014&utm_medium=email&utm_source=newsletter&ET=healthdatamanagement%3Ae2798061%3A3722191a%3A&st=email.

Goth, G. 2014b. FDA approves chair sensor for patient monitoring. *Health Data Management*, July. Retrieved from http://www.healthdatamanagement.com/news/FDA-Approves-Chair-Sensor-for-Patient-Monitoring-48372-1.html?utm_campaign=daily-jul%208%202014&utm_medium=email&utm_source=newsletter&ET=healthdatamanagement%3Ae2804746%3A3722191a%3A&st=email.

Goth, G. 2014c. Tool to predict cardiac risk for rheumatoid arthritis patients. *Health Data Management*, June. Retrieved from http://www.healthdatamanagement.com/news/Tool-to-Predict-Cardiac-Risk-for-Rheumatoid-Arthritis-Patients-48250-1.html?utm_campaign=daily-jun%2018%20

2014&utm_medium=email&utm_source=newsletter&ET=health
datamanagement%3Ae2750089%3A3722191a%3A&st=email.

Goth, G. 2014d. Gaming physicians better control patient blood
pressure. *Health Data Management*, May. Retrieved from
http://www.healthdatamanagement.com/news/Gaming-
Physicians-Better-Control-Patient-Blood-Pressure-48127-1.
html?utm_campaign=daily-may%2028%202014&utm_
medium=email&utm_source=newsletter&ET=healthdatamanage
ment%3Ae2691114%3A3722191a%3A&st=email.

Goth, G. 2014e. Game theory helping to predict cancer progress.
Health Data Management. Retrieved from http://www.
healthdatamanagement.com/news/Game-Theory-Helping-to-
Predict-Cancer-Progress-48490-1.html.

Goth, G. 2014f. UCLA surgeons use Google Glass for remote
training. *Health Data Management*, June. Retrieved from
http://www.healthdatamanagement.com/news/UCLA-
Surgeons-Use-Google-Glass-for-Remote-Training-48242-1.
html?utm_campaign=daily-jun%2017%202014&utm_
medium=email&utm_source=newsletter&ET=healthdatamanage
ment%3Ae2746869%3A3722191a%3A&st=email.

Goth, G. 2014g. Web-based counseling a cost-effective approach
for heart disease. *Health Data Management*, May. Retrieved
from http://www.healthdatamanagement.com/news/Web-
Based-Counseling-Cuts-Costs-Risk-of-Heart-Disease-48142-1.
html?utm_campaign=daily-may%2031%202014&utm_
medium=email&utm_source=newsletter&ET=healthdatamanage
ment%3Ae2701214%3A3722191a%3A&st=email.

Gownder, J. P. 2013. Wearables will reshape the way enterprises
work. *Computerworld*, November 18. Retrieved from
http://www.cio.com/article/print/743389.

Grande, D. 2014. Penn study shows health policy researchers
lack confidence in social media for communicating scientific
evidence. Penn Medicine, June 10. Retrieved from http://www.
uphs.upenn.edu/news/News_Releases/2014/06/grande/.

Gregg, H. 2014a. Cleveland Clinic's app development strategy:
"Never consider a project finished." *Becker's Hospital Review*,
May 5. Retrieved from http://www.beckershospitalreview.com/
healthcare-information-technology/cleveland-clinic-s-app-
development-strategy-never-consider-a-project-finished.html.

Gregg, H. 2014b. A CISO's biggest challenge. *Becker's Hospital Review*, June 27. Retrieved from http://www.beckershospitalreview. com/healthcare-information-technology/a-ciso-s-biggest-challenge. html.

Gregg, H. 2014c. How data leaks are compromising hospitals' medical devices. *Becker's Hospital Review*, June 26. Retrieved from http://www.beckershospitalreview.com/healthcare-information-technology/how-data-leaks-are-compromising-hospitals-medical-devices.html.

Halamka, J. 2014. Wearable computing at BICMC. *Healthcare IT News*, March 12. Retrieved from http://www.healthcareitnews. com/blog/wearable-computing-bidmc?single-page=true.

Hall, S. 2014. Deloitte: Global eVisits to reach 100 million by year's end. Fierce Health IT, August 12. Retrieved from http:// www.fiercehealthit.com/story/deloitte-global-evisits-reach-100-million-years-end/2014-08-12?utm_medium=nl&utm_source=internal.

Harvard Business Report. 2014. The digital dividend: The first mover advantage. Verizon Enterprise. Retrieved from http:// www.verizonenterprise.com/resources/reports/rp_hbr-digital-dividend-first-mover-advantage_en_xg.pdf.

Hay, T. 2014. Ad-Tech entrepreneurs build cancer database. *The Wall Street Journal*, June 18. Retrieved from http:// online.wsj.com/articles/ad-tech-entrepreneurs-build-cancer-database-1403134613.

Health and Human Services. 2014a. Revisions to payment policies. Fed. Reg. Doc. 2014-15948, July 7, 2014. Retrieved from https://s3.amazonaws.com/public-inspection.federalregister.gov/2014-15948.pdf.

Health and Human Services. 2014b. Proposed health IT strategy aims to promote innovation, protect patients, and avoid regulatory duplication. U.S. FDA, April 3. Retrieved from http:// www.fda.gov/NewsEvents/Newsroom/PressAnnouncements/ucm390988.htm.

Hoadley, K. A., Yau, C., Wolf, D. M., Cherniak, A. D., Tamborero, D., Ng, S., Leiserson, M. D. M., Beifang, N., McLellan, M. D., Uzanangelov, V., Zhang, J., Kandoth, C., Akbani, R., Hui, S., Omberg, L., Chu, A., Margolin, A. A., van't Veer, L. J., Lopez-Bigas, N., Laird, P. W., Raphael, B. J., Ding, L., Robertson, G., Byers, L. A., Mills, G. B., Weinstein, J. N., Van Waes, C., Zhon, C., Collisson, E. A., Benz, C. C., Perou, C. M., and Stuart, J. M. 2014. The cancer genome atlas research network: Multiplatform analysis of 12 cancer. *Cell* 158(4). Retrieved from http://www.cell.com/cell/fulltext/S0092-8674%2814%2900876-9#.

Hodge, N. 2014. 5 steps to get payers and providers to tap mHealth apps. *mHealth News*, June 30. Retrieved from http://www.mhealthnews.com/news/5-steps-get-payers-and-providers-tap-mhealth-apps-mobile-diabetes-Medicaid-ACOs.

Hotz, R. B. 2014. Man-made DNA opens doors. *The Wall Street Journal*, May 7. Retrieved from http://online.wsj.com/news/articles/SB10001424052702304431104579547673907525130?mg=reno64-wsj.

Inagaiki, K. 2014. Nikon to pursue medical-device acquisitions. *The Wall Street Journal*, June 18. Retrieved from http://online.wsj.com/news/articles/SB20001424052702304292904579629900603699912.

Iskowitz, M. 2014. Sifting social media for the "why" behind Rx switching. MM&M, June 23. Retrieved from http://www.mmm-online.com/sifting-social-media-for-the-why-behind-rx-switching/article/357207/.

Jain, S. 2014. How to make healthcare innovation work in the real world—Merck's partnership with patients like me. MM&M, July 8. Retrieved from http://www.mmm-online.com/how-to-make-healthcare-innovation-work-in-the-real-worldmercks-partnership-with-patientslikeme/article/359789/?DCMP=EMC-MMM_WeeklyDigest&spMailingID=9003225&spUserID=MTIxMTQ4MjczMTgwS0&spJobID=340914836&spReportId=MzQwOTE0ODM2S0.

Janeczko, L. L. 2014. What's next in healthcare mobile apps? Spit into your phone to know if you're stressed. *MedCity News*, July. Retrieved from http://medcitynews.com/2014/07/whats-next-healthcare-mobile-apps-spit-phone-know-youre-stressed/#ixzz36hYu3sIe.

Javitt, J. 2014. Case study: Using mHealth to manage diabetes. *mHealth News*. Retrieved from http://www.mhealthnews.com/print/24916.

Jayanthi, A. 2014a. 7 statistics on mHealth apps consumer use. *Becker's Hospital Review*, June 23. Retrieved from http://www.beckershospitalreview.com/healthcare-information-technology/7-statistics-on-mhealth-app-consumer-use.html.

Jayanthi, A. 2014b. Telemedicine's ROI: Maricopa integrated health system posts 77.8%. Retrieved from http://www.beckershospital review.com/healthcare-information-technology/telemedicine-s-roi-maricopa-integrated-health-system-posts-77-8.html.

Jayanthi, A. 2014c. The rise of mHealth: 10 trends. *Becker's Hospital Review*, June 27. Retrieved from http://www.beckershospital review.com/healthcare-information-technology/the-rise-of-mhealth-10-trends.html.

Johnson, S. R. 2014. Nonsurgical heart valve procedure spurs cost concerns. *Modern Healthcare*. 44(13)12.

Kahn, A. 2014. What to look for in a fitness app. *U.S. News and World Report*, July 18. Retrieved from http://health.usnews.com/health-news/health-wellness/articles/2014/07/18/what-to-look-for-in-a-fitness-app.

Keenan, J. 2014. MIT device could give arthritics and others a helping hand with extra fingers. Fierce Medical Devices, July 21. Retrieved from http://www.fiercemedicaldevices.com/story/mit-device-could-give-arthritics-and-others-helping-hand-extra-fingers/2014-07-21?utm_medium=nl&utm_source=internal.

Keshavan, M. 2014a. British wound care company starting clinical trials to bring tests to U.S. *MedCity News*, July 12. Retrieved from http://medcitynews.com/2014/07/british-wound-care-co-starting-clinical-trials-bring-tests-u-s/#ixzz37G0WA8Kl.

Keshavan, M. 2014b. Epibone helps patients grow their own bone. *MedCity News*, August 13. Retrieved from http://medcitynews.com/2014/08/epibone/#ixzz3AMp1mvCE.

Kim, J. 2013. Automated diagnostics: How supercomputers fit in radiology's future. TechTarget. Retrieved from http://search healthit.techtarget.com/feature/Automated-diagnostics-How-supercomputers-fit-in-radiologys-future?src=5226419&asrc=EM_ERU_27616933&uid=16343684&utm_medium=EM&utm_source=ERU&utm_campaign=20140327_ERU+Transmission+for+03%2F27%2F2014+%28UserUniverse%3A+750240%29_myka-reports%40techtarget.com.

Kitchens, B., Harle, C. A., and Li, S. 2012. Quality of online search results. *ScienceDirect*, November 6. Retrieved from http://dx.doi.org/10.1016/j.dss.2012.10.050.

Knight, M. 2014. 3-D printing is revolutionizing surgery. *Modern Healthcare*, March 24. Retrieved from http://www.modern

healthcare.com/article/20140324/INFO/303249992?AllowView=
VDl3UXk1TzZDUENCbXgzS0M0M3hlMENyaTBVZEErUT0=
&utm_source=link-20140324-INFO-303249992&utm_
medium=email&utm_campaign=hits&utm_name=top.

Knight, E. P. and Shea, K. 2014. A patient-focused framework
integrating self-management and informatics. *Journal of Nursing
Scholarship* 46(2)91–97.

Koetsier, J. 2013. Wearable tech pioneer Interaxon closes $6M series
A for its brain-sensing Muse headband. *VentureBeat*, August 15.
Retrieved from http://venturebeat.com/2013/08/15/wearable-
tech-pioneer-interaxon-closes-6m-series-a-for-its-brain-sensing-
muse-headband/.

Kolata, G. 2014. In single gene, a path to fight heart attacks. *The
New York Times*, June 19. Retrieved from http://www.nytimes.
com/2014/06/19/health/scientists-identify-mutations-that-
protect-against-heart-attacks.html?

Kontos, E., Blake, K. D., Chou, W. S., and Prestin, A. 2014. Predictors
of eHealth usage: Insights on the digital divide from the health
information national trends survey 2012. *J Med Internet Res*
2014:16(7):e172. Retrieved from *JMIR* http://www.jmir.org/
2014/7/e172/.

Landro, E. 2014. Interactive video helps patients get access to
medical specialists. *The Wall Street Journal*, May 12. Retrieved
from http://online.wsj.com/news/articles/SB1000142405270230
4081804579557770525373400?mg=reno64-wsj#.

Lee, S. M. 2013. Augmedix raises $3.2 million to bring Google Glass
into doctor's office. *SFGate*, March 19. Retrieved from http://
blog.sfgate.com/techchron/2014/03/19/augmedix-raises-3-2-
million-to-bring-google-glass-into-doctors-office/.

Lee, D. 2014. Why clinical trials need mobile health tools. *mHealth
News*, January 15. Retrieved from http://www.mhealthnews.
com/blog/why-clinical-trials-need-mobile-health-tools?single-
page=true.

Leventhal, R. 2014. Leveraging telehealth for sleep apnea patients
at MedBridge Healthcare. Healthcare Informatics, June 19.
Retrieved from http://www.healthcare-informatics.com/
article/leveraging-telehealth-sleep-apnea-patients-medbridge-
healthcare?WA_MAILINGLEVEL_CODE=&spMailingID=46327
831&spUserID=NTA3NzI0OTAxMzkS1&spJobID=463544580&
spReportId=NDYzNTQ0NTgwS0.

Lobo, S. 2014. New rotator cuff repair technique uses dissolving scaffold + special staples. *MedCity News*, May 29. Retrieved from http://medcitynews.com/2014/05/new-surgery-rotator-cuff-injuries/#ixzz33IzXFjs5.

Lopes, A. 2014. IBM to offer iPads and iPhones for business users. *Reuters*, July 16. Retrieved from http://in.reuters.com/article/2014/07/15/us-ibm-apple-partnership-idINKBN0FK2NG 20140715.

Lovrien, K., Petersen, L. C., and Pierce, J. 2014. The virtual primary healthcare revolution: What health systems need to know. *Becker's Hospital Review*, February 3. Retrieved from http://www.beckershospitalreview.com/strategic-planning/the-virtual-primary-healthcare-revolution-what-health-systems-need-to-know.html.

Lynch, W. 2014. 4 key measures of patient engagement. *Healthcare Finance News*, April 10. Retrieved from http://www.healthcare-financenews.com/news/4-key-measures-patient-engagement.

MacDougall, R. 2014. New report offers a primer for doctors' use of clinical genome and exome sequencing. National Institutes of Health, June 18. Retrieved from http://www.nih.gov/news/health/jun2014/nhgri-18.htm.

Mace, S. 2014a. Sports medicine turns to telemedicine. *HealthLeaders Media*, April 29. Retrieved from http://www.healthleadersmedia.com/print/TEC-303894/Sports-Medicine-Turns-to-Telemedicine.

Mace, S. 2014b. Developing telemedicine options. *HealthLeaders* 17(3)40–42.

Mace, S. 2014c. The Internet of things is enabling healthcare leaders to achieve objectives through better collection and reporting of data. *HealthLeaders Media*, June. Retrieved from http://www.health leadersmedia.com/print/TEC-305370/Healthcare-Embedded-and-Connected.

Mace, S. 2014d. Personalized medicine meets EHR integration at Mt. Sinai. *HealthLeaders Media*, July 15. Retrieved from http://www.healthleadersmedia.com/print/TEC-306371/Personalized-Medicine-Meets-EHR-Integration-at-Mt-Sinai.

Manos, D. 2014. Many docs at high risk for MU penalties. *Healthcare IT News*, June 26. Retrieved from http://www.healthcare itnews.com/news/many-docs-high-risk-mu-penalties.

McCann, E. 2013. mHealth enters consumer golden age. *Healthcare IT News*, October 25. Retrieved from http://www.healthcareit-news.com/news/mhealth-enters-consumer-golden-age?topic=16.

McCann, E. 2014a. Telehealth takes off in rural areas. *Healthcare IT News*, February 4. Retrieved from http://www.healthcareitnews. com/news/telehealth-takes-nationwide.

McCann, E. 2014b. Healthcare security stuck in the stone age. *Healthcare IT News*, April 22. Retrieved from http://www. healthcareitnews.com/news/healthcare-security-stuck-stone-age?topic=16,17,18.

McCann, E. 2014c. What's really driving telehealth? Retrieved from http://www.mhealthnews.com/news/whats-really-driving-telehealth-mobile-mHealth-ATA.

McCann, E. 2014d. Boston Children's innovation showcase. *Healthcare IT News*, April 9. Retrieved from http://www. healthcareitnews.com/slideshow/boston-childrens-innovation-showcase?page=2.

McCann, E. 2014e. Security: Healthcare's fixer-upper. *Healthcare IT News*, June 4. Retrieved from http://www.healthcareitnews. com/news/security-healthcares-fixer-upper.

McCann, E. 2014f. What HIPAA does not cover. *Healthcare IT News*, July 16. Retrieved from http://www.healthcareitnews.com/ news/what-hipaa-doesnt-cover?topic=06,18&mkt_tok=3RkMMJ WWfF9wsRonuq%2FJZKXonjHpfsX66%2BQqULHr08Yy0EZ5Vu nJEUWy2YIETNQ%2FcOedCQkZHblFnVUKSK2vULcNqKwP.

Medical Devices. 2013. Mobile Medical Devices. U.S. Food and Drug Administration. Retrieved from http://www.fda.gov/ medicaldevices/productsandmedicalprocedures/connected health/mobilemedicalapplications/default.htm.

Meek, T. 2014. ADA: Merck launches registry for type 2 diabetes. PMLive, June 17. Retrieved from http://www.pmlive.com/ pharma_news/ada_merck_launches_registry_for_type_2_ diabetes_578567.

Mehrotra, A., Paone, S., Martich, G. D., Albert, S., and Shevchik, G. 2013. A comparison of care at e-visits and physician office visits for sinusitis and urinary tract infection. *Jama Internal Medicine* 173(1). Retrieved from http://archinte.jamanetwork. com/article.aspx?articleID=1392490.

Melnick, M. 2014. A new smartphone app could detect mental illness just from hearing your voice. *Huffington Post*, May 8. Retrieved from http://www.huffingtonpost.com/2014/05/08/ smartphone-app-bipolar_n_5281578.html.

Meneghetti, A. 2014. Clinical innovation for uncertainty in the moments of care. Aetna Health, May 29. Retrieved from http://

www.athenahealth.com/blog/2014/05/29/clinical-innovation-uncertainty-moments-care/?cmp=10028619.

Millard, M. 2014a. Brainwave technology breakthrough? *Healthcare IT News*, August 6. Retrieved from http://www.healthcareitnews.com/news/brainwave-technology-breakthrough.

Millard, M. 2014b. Cardiac patients taking PHRs to heart. *Healthcare IT News*, June 10. Retrieved from http://www.healthcareitnews.com/news/cardiac-patients-taking-phrs-heart?single-page=true.

Millard, M. 2014c. For portals, speak patients' language. *Healthcare IT News*, June 25. Retrieved from http://www.healthcareitnews.com/news/portals-speak-patients-language?single-page=true.

Millard, M. and McCann, E. 2014. "Most Wired" 2014 hospitals big on data. *Healthcare IT News*, July 9. Retrieved from http://www.healthcareitnews.com/news/most-wired-2014-named?topic=08,16,17&mkt_tok=3RkMMJWWfF9wsRonuq3BZK XonjHpfsXw7%2BUrWLHr08Yy0EZ5VunJEUWy2YICSNQ%2FcO edCQkZHblFnVUKSK2vULcNqKwP.

MobilityWOD. 2014. Retrieved from http://www.mobilitywod.com/dailyrx/#.

Mobiquity. 2014. Get mobile, get healthy: The application of health and fitness. Mobiquity. Retrieved from http://www.mobiquity inc.com/get-mobile-get-healthy-appification-health-fitness-report?registered=true&sid=219.

Modern Healthcare. Associated Press. 2014. L.A. doctors practice speeding up trauma care. *Modern Healthcare*, March 25. Retrieved from http://www.modernhealthcare.com/article/20140325/INFO/303259977?AllowView=VDl3UXk1TzZD UEdCbXgzS0M0M3hlMENyaWtVZERlRT0=&utm_source=link-20140325-INFO-303259977&utm_medium=email&utm_campaign=hits&utm_name=top.

Monegain, B. 2013. Mayo robot to flag gridiron concussions. *Healthcare IT News*, September 3. Retrieved from http://www.healthcareitnews.com/news/mayoclinic-robot-flag-gridiron-concussions?single-page=true.

Morrissey, J. 2014. UnitedHealth CEO sees a powerful future for telehealth. *H&HN Daily*, May 20. Retrieved from http://www.hhnmag.com/display/HHN-news-article.dhtml?dcrPath=/templatedata/HF_Common/NewsArticle/data/HHN/Daily/2014/May/052014-morrissey-telehealth-health-IT.

Mullarky, C. 2014. Walking 12,000 steps a day neutralizes negative effects of fructose. Consultant 360, September 15. Retrieved from http://www.consultant360.com/exclusives/walking-12000-steps-day-neutralizes-negative-effects-fructose.

NACHA. 2014. The Electronics Payments Association. Retrieved from https://www.nacha.org/content/industry-needs.

Naik, G. 2014a. Breakthrough in quest to grow body parts: Lab-made vaginas transplanted into patients whose own were absent due to rare disease. *The Wall Street Journal*, April 10. Retrieved from http://online.wsj.com/news/articles/SB10001424052702303603904579493682196167594?KEYWORDS=vagina&mg=reno64-wsj.

Naik, G. 2014b. Gene therapy corrects irregular heartbeat. *The Wall Street Journal*, July 16. Retrieved from http://online.wsj.com/articles/gene-therapy-corrects-irregular-heartbeat-in-pigs-1405533603.

Netburn, D. 2014. Freaking out about a minor medical procedure? Video glasses can help. *LA Times*, March 24. Retrieved from http://www.latimes.com/science/sciencenow/la-sci-sn-video-glasses-stress-20140324,0,879602.story.

Neuhauser, A. 2014. Health care harnesses social media. *US News & World Report*, June 5. Retrieved from http://www.usnews.com/news/articles/2014/06/05/health-care-harnesses-social-media.

O'Donnell, J. 2014. Feds push electronic records that make fraud easier. *USA Today*, July 6. Retrieved from http://www.usatoday.com/story/news/nation/2014/07/06/electronic-health-records-medicare-healthcare-fraud-funding/12157645/?utm_campaign=KHN%3A+First+Edition&utm_source=hs_email&utm_medium=email&utm_content=13387764&_hsenc=p2ANqtz-90LXYd__UaLmgWg-2RvXagJCV3LwLtRQ5tjGgUPFHvnfbv8YKze0ULEhhmaRfrFR3oUadM2IcHsUxuDpIrfcrBw-6uqflBSzKUveAlLum7r6EftmA&_hsmi=13387764.

Olson, P. 2014. Exclusive: Google wants to collect your health data with "Google Fit." *Forbes*, June 12. Retrieved from http://www.forbes.com/sites/parmyolson/2014/06/12/exclusive-google-to-launch-health-service-google-fit-at-developers-conference/.

Optum. 2014. Moneyball analytics. Health Forum. Retrieved from http://www.healthforum.com/whitepapers/index.dhtml.

Ottenhoff, M. 2012. Infographic: Rising use of social and mobile in healthcare. *SparkReport*, December 17. Retrieved from http://thesparkreport.com/infographic-social-mobile-healthcare/.

Owlett Press Release. 2013. *UTAH Business*, September 4. Retrieved http://www.utahbusiness.com/articles/view/owlet_baby_care_introduces_wearable_infant_monitor.

Page, D. 2014. Telemed system speeds stroke care. *H&HN*, April 8. Retrieved from http://www.hhnmag.com/display/HHN-news-article.dhtml?dcrPath=/templatedata/HF_Common/NewsArticle/data/HHN/Magazine/2014/Apr/inbox-the-hookup&utm_source=daily&utm_medium=email&utm_campaign=HHN&utm_source=Daily&utm_medium=email&utm_campaign=general.

Pai, A. 2014. Kaiser Permanente app passes 1M downloads. *Mobihealth News*, June 4. Retrieved from http://mobihealthnews.com/33817/kaiser-permanente-app-passes-1m-downloads/.

Parks Associates. 2014. Almost 30% of broadband households own, use connected health device. Parks Associates, February 25. Retrieved from http://www.parksassociates.com/blog/article/pr-feb2014-mcw.

Pecci, A. W. 2014a. Tagging, tracking nurses improves workflow. *HealthLeaders Media*, March 25. Retrieved from http://www.healthleadersmedia.com/page-5/NRS-302215/Tagging-Tracking-Nurses-Improves-Workflow##.

Pecci, A. W. 2014b. Fall prevention study focuses on wearable sensors. *HealthLeaders Media*, May 20. Retrieved from http://www.healthleadersmedia.com/print/NRS-304674/Fall-Prevention-Study-Focuses-on-Wearable-Sensors.

Pender, C. 2014. Mississippi leading telehealth research, policy push. *The Clarion Ledger*, April 22. Retrieved from http://www.clarionledger.com/story/news/2014/04/22/mississippi-leading-telehealth-research-policy-push/8034685/.

Penn Medicine. 2014. Penn Medicine stroke experts identify geographic and gender disparities among stroke patients, demonstrate new app to optimize acute stroke care. Penn Medicine, April 28. Retrieved from http://www.uphs.upenn.edu/news/News_Releases/2014/04/stroke/.

Penoza, C. 2014. Mayday! Mayday! Bitpipe, May. Retrieved from http://www.bitpipe.com/data/demandEngage.action?resId=1398972130_664.

Phillips, S. 2014. FDA to host Addictive Manufacturing Workshop and debate regulation, September 4. *Inside 3DP*. Retrieved from http://www.inside3dp.com/fda-host-additive-manufacturing-workshop-debate-regulation/.

Pittman, D. 2014. Big cyber hack of health records is "only a matter of time." *Politico*, July 1. Retrieved from http://www.politico.com/story/2014/07/cyber-hack-health-records-matter-time-108486.html#ixzz36K2qbwGQ.

Pogoreic, D. 2014a. Way beyond a watch: Sensor + app + bracelet combo is the future of wearables. *MedCity News*, March 19. Retrieved from http://medcitynews.com/2014/03/design-firms-epilepsy-management-concept-gives-glimpse-health-wearables-headed/#ixzz2wnNtGwbw.

Pogoreic, D. 2014b. Biochip mimics how the body produces platelets so they could be made in a lab. Research2Guidance. Retrieved from http://research2guidance.com/r2g/mHealth-App-Developer-Economics-2014.pdf zzzzzhttp://medcitynews.com/2014/04/biochip-mimcs-body-produces-platelets-address-challenges-platelet-transfusions/#ixzz2zWNqZFYf.

Pogoreic, D. 2014c. Spark Therapeutics' late-stage gene therapy for inherited blindness takes a $73M step forward. *MedCity News*, May 27. Retrieved from http://medcitynews.com/2014/05/gene-therapy-inherited-blindness/#ixzz331NjN64j.

Porteus. 2014. Digital health feedback system. Porteus. Retrieved from http://porteus.com/technology/digital-health system.

Quinn, C. 2014. Online platform connects doctors separated by distance, expertise. *WGBH News*, April 23. Retrieved from http://wgbhnews.org/post/online-platform-connects-doctors-separated-distance-expertise.

Reader, R. 2014. When Angry Birds and robots are involved, kids with disabilities engage more in rehabilitation. *MedCity News*, July. Retrieved http://medcitynews.com/2014/07/robots-can-play-angry-birds-help-kids-disabilities/#ixzz37GBEjeFI.

Research2guidance. 2014. mHealth app developer economics 2014. Research2Guidance. Retrieved from http://research2guidance.com/r2g/mHealth-App-Developer-Economics-2014.pdf.

Robinson, F., Schechner, S., and Mizroch, A. 2014. EU orders Google to let users erase past. *The Wall Street Journal*, May 13. Retrieved from http://online.wsj.com/news/articles/SB10001424052702303851804579559280623224964?KEYWORDS=facebook+and+ europe&mg=reno64-wsj.

Rodriguez, G. 2014. Advances in medical imaging allow the scan to fit the patient. *MedCity News*, July 12. Retrieved from http://medcitynews.com/2014/07/tailoring-patient-care-medical-imaging-innovations/#ixzz37G5ZjuJI.

Rojann, S. Y. 2014. DNA-based research may have unveiled long-sought diabetes treatment. *MIT Technology Review*, May 23. Retrieved from http://www.technologyreview.com/news/527396/dna-based-research-may-have-unveiled-long-sought-diabetes-treatment/.

Ronanki, R. and Steier, D. 2014. Tech Trends 2014. UK: Deloitte University Press. Retrieved from http://d2mtr37y39tpbu.cloudfront.net/wp-content/uploads/2014/02/Tech-Trends-2014_FINAL-ELECTRONIC_single.2.24.pdf.

Rosman, K. 2014. Wearable "smart" shirt maker OMSignal raises $10 million. *The Wall Street Journal*, June 24. Retrieved from http://blogs.wsj.com/venturecapital/2014/06/24/wearable-smart-shirt-maker-omsignal-raises-10-million/.

Roston, M. 2014. New offering for job seekers: Fewer embarrassing social media photos. *The New York Times*, June 21. Retrieved from http://bits.blogs.nytimes.com/2014/06/21/a-way-to-rid-your-social-media-of-embarrassments/?_php=true&_type=blogs&_php=true&_type=blogs&pagewanted=all&_r=1&.

Rowe, J. 2013. 3 ways IT helps spine care, research. *HealthLeaders Media*, Retrieved from http://www.healthleadersmedia.com/print/NRS-302215/Tagging-Tracking-Nurses-Improves-Workflow http://www.healthcareitnews.com/news/3-ways-it-helps-spine-care-research?single-page=true.

Rudderham, T. 2014. How the Oculus Rift helped Roberta Firstenberg battle cancer. The Rift Arcade, April 17. Retrieved from http://www.theriftarcade.com/how-the-oculus-rift-helped-roberta-firstenberg-battle-cancer/.

Ruhe, N. 2014a. Ohio State and Battelle help paralyzed people move again by just thinking about it. *MedCity News*, June 28. Retrieved from http://medcitynews.com/2014/06/paralyzed-can-move-just-thinking/#ixzz362cj7vRv.

Ruhe, N. 2014b. Motion capture technology + mobile app makes fake feet work more like real ones. *MedCity News*, July 12. Retrieved from http://medcitynews.com/2014/07/motion-capture-technologymobile-app-make-even-easier-people-lower-limb-prosthetics-get-mobile/#ixzz37G7xBSdI.

Ruhe, N. 2014c. 3D printing is straightening out scoliosis by building braces kids will actually wear. *MedCity News*, June 19. Retrieved from http://medcitynews.com/2014/06/3d-printing-straightening-medical-world-better-back-braces-help-treat-scoliosis/#ixzz35D332jBj.

Russell, K. 2014. Fitness apps growing 87% faster than the overall app market. TechCrunch, June 19. Retrieved from http://techcrunch.com/2014/06/19/fitness-app-usage-is-growing-87-faster-than-the-overall-app-market/.

Sarvastani, A. 2014. Samsung dives into digital health with wearable sensor, $50M fund. Mass Device, May 29. Retrieved from http://www.massdevice.com/news/samsung-dives-digital-health-with-open-platforms-50m-fund?page=show.

Saxena, V. 2014a. Wearable biosensor for assessing back injuries wins FDA clearance. Fierce Medical Devices, July 17. Retrieved from http://www.fiercemedicaldevices.com/story/wearable-biosensor-assessing-back-injuries-wins-fda-clearance/2014-07-17?utm_medium=nl&utm_source=internal.

Saxena, V. 2014b. FDA approves expandable implant for spinal fusion surgery. Fierce Medical Devices, July 21. Retrieved from http://www.fiercemedicaldevices.com/story/fda-clears-expandable-implant-spinal-fusion-surgery/2014-07-21?utm_medium=nl&utm_source=internal.

Saxena, V. 2014c. Experts tell HHS to integrate UDI into insurance claims. Fierce Medical Devices, June 12. Retrieved from http://www.fiercemedicaldevices.com/story/experts-tell-hhs-integrate-udi-insurance-claims/2014-06-12#ixzz34RrpHA9D.

Saxena, V. 2014d. FDA clears first smartphone-based device to detect atrial fibrillation. Fierce Medical Devices, August 22. Retrieved from http://www.fiercemedicaldevices.com/story/fda-clears-alivecor-smartphone-plug-heartmonitor-detect-atrial-fibrillatio/2014-08-22.

Schwartz, E. 2014a. mHealth startups hone in on evidence based medicine. *mHealth News,* May 12. Retrieved from http://www.mhealthnews.com/news/mhealth-startups-home-evidence-based-medicine.

Schwartz, E. 2014b. Spotlight on: Care transition technologies. *mHealth News,* May 27. Retrieved from http://www.mhealthnews.com/news/spotlight-care-transition-technologies?single-page=true.

Schwartz, E. 2014c. Could gamification be a secret to cutting costs? *mHealth News,* January 27. Retrieved from http://www.mhealthnews.com/news/gamification-secret-cutting-care-costs-mHealth-mobile.

Scientific Blogging. 2014. New data suggests relationship between diet and arthritis. *Science 2.0,* June 11. Retrieved from http:// www.science20.com/news_articles/

new_data_suggests_relationship_between_diet_and_
arthritis-138310.

Scriplogix. 2014. Patient activation platform. Scriplogix. Retrieved
from 22.scriplogix.com.

Selvam, A. 2013. The social media scene: Helping the uninsured
log on so they can sign up. *Modern Healthcare*, October
26. Retrieved from http://www.modernhealthcare.com/
article/20131026/MAGAZINE/310269933.

Singer, N. 2014. When a health plan knows how you shop. *The
New York Times*, June 28. Retrieved from http://www.nytimes.
com/2014/06/29/technology/when-a-health-plan-knows-how-
you-shop.html?emc=edit_th_20140629&nl=todaysheadlines&
nlid=7766146&_r=0.

Slabodkin, G. 2014a. Voxiva digital health programs surpass
1 million users. Health Data Management. Retrieved from
http://www.healthdatamanagement.com/news/Voxiva-
Digital-Health-Programs-Surpass-One-Million-Users-48037-1.
html?zkPrintable=true.

Slabodkin, G. 2014b. FDA approves wireless device to remotely
monitor CHF patients. Health Data Management. Retrieved
from http://www.healthdatamanagement.com/news/
FDA-Approves-Wireless-Device-to-Remotely-Monitor-CHF-
Patients-48149-1.html?utm_campaign=daily-may%2031%20
2014&utm_medium=email&utm_source=newsletter&ET=health
datamanagement%3Ae2701214%3A3722191a%3A&st=email.

Slepin, R. 2014. CHIME time: Engaging patients as consumers.
Modern Healthcare, March 28. Retrieved from http://www.
modernhealthcare.com/article/20140328/NEWS/303289952?
AllowView=VDl3UXk1TzZDUHlCbkJiYkY0M3hlMENyaDBVZE
QrUT0=&utm_source=link-20140328-NEWS-303289952&utm_
medium=email&utm_campaign=hits&utm_name=top.

Smith, A. 2014. Older adults and technology use. Pew
Research, April 3. Retrieved from http://www.pewinternet.
org/2014/04/03/older-adults-and-technology-use/.

Somerville, H. 2014. The doctor will see you now—On a smartphone.
San Jose Mercury News, August 8. Retrieved from http://www.
mercurynews.com/business/ci_26295004/doctor-will-nowsee-you-
smartphone.

Soo, Z. 2014. Giraffe Friend is a wearable to help you sit up straight.
MedCity News, April. Retrieved from http://medcitynews.com/
2014/04/giraffe-friend-wearable-help-sit-straight/#ixzz2zGtH9xxX.

Stern, J. 2014. Like a mom, bracelet nags you at the beach. *Imarket-reports*, June 10. Retrieved from http://imarketreports.com/like-a-mom-bracelet-nags-you-at-the-beach.html.

Su, C. J. 2013. Personal rehabilitation exercise assistant with kinect and dynamic time warping. *International Journal of Information and Education Technology*, 3 (4) pp. 448–454.

Sullivan, M. 2014a. Pocket-sized digital glucose meter from iHealth sends readings via a phone's headphone jack. *MedCity News*, June. Retrieved from http://medcitynews.com/2014/06/pocket-sized-digital-glucose-meter-ihealth-plugs/#ixzz34ccFhQcc.

Sullivan, M. 2014b. Intel wearables chief reacts to Apple, Samsung health data platforms: "Who owns the data?" *MedCity News*, June. Retrieved from http://medcitynews.com/2014/06/intel-wearables-chief-unimpressed-apple-samsung-uber-platforms/#ixzz33rI1R0Hl.

Sullivan, M. 2014c. FTC may soon turn its regulatory gaze toward data-collecting health apps. *VentureBeat*, May 16. Retrieved from http://venturebeat.com/2014/05/16/ftc-may-soon-turn-its-regulatory-gaze-toward-data-collecting-health-apps/.

Sullivan, M. 2014d. Watson + Siri: New mHealth power couple? *Healthcare IT News*, July 16. Retrieved from http://www.healthcareitnews.com/news/watson-siri-new-mhealth-power-couple?topic=76,16,26&mkt_tok=3RkMMJWWfF9wsRonuq%2FJ ZKXonjHpfsX66%2BQqULHr08Yy0EZ5VunJEUWy2YIETNQ%2F cOedCQkZHblFnVUKSK2vULcNqKwP.

Tabuchi, H. 2014. In advent of the smartwatch, a name that's been there before. *The New York Times*, August 27. Retrieved from http://www.nytimes.com/2013/08/28/technology/in-advent-of-the-smartwatch-a-name-thats-been-there-before.html.

Theilst, C. 2012. Leveraging emerging technologies for improved patient engagement and safety. iHealthBeat, November 6. Retrieved from http://www.ihealthbeat.org/perspectives/2012/leveraging-emerging-technologies-for-improved-patient-engagement-and-safety.

Thomas, J. D. 2013. When your food bites back, Twitter trackers will know. *Modern Healthcare*. 34(42)44.

Thomas, L. and Capistrant, G. 2014. State telemedicine gaps analysis. Coverage & reimbursement. American Telemedicine Association. Retrieved from http://www.americantelemed.org/docs/default-source/policy/50-state-telemedicine-gaps-analysis-coverage-and-reimbursement.pdf?sfvrsn=6.

Topol, E. 2014a. The paradox of technology bolstering the doctor-patient relationship. *H&HN Daily*, May 27. Retrieved from http://www.hhnmag.com/display/HHN-news-article. dhtml?dcrPath=/templatedata/HF_Common/NewsArticle/data/HHN/Daily/2014/Mar/032714-topol-mhealth&utm_source=Daily&utm_medium=email&utm_campaign=general.

Topol, E. 2014b. How breathing and speaking into your smartphone may be transformative. *H&HN Daily*, April 17. Retrieved from http://www.hhnmag.com/display/HHN-news-article.dhtml?dcrPath=/templatedata/HF_Common/NewsArticle/data/HHN/Daily/2014/Apr/041714-topol-connectingthecontinuum&utm_source=Daily&utm_medium=email&utm_campaign=general.

Tran, E., Turcotte, S., Gros, A., Robbins, P. F., Lu, Y. C., Dudley, M. E., Wunderlich, J. R., Somerville, R. P., Hogan, K., Hinrichs, C. S., Parkhurst, M. R., Yang, J. C., and Rosenberg. S. A. 2014. Cancer immunotherapy based on mutation-specific CD4+ T cells in a patient with epithelial cancer. *Science*, May 9; 344(6184): 641–5. doi: 10.1126/science.1251102. PMID: 24812403.

Uddin, M., Tammimies, K., Pellecchia, G., Alipanahi, B., Hu, P., Wang, Z., Pinto, D., Lau, L., Nalpathamkalam, T., Marshall, C. R., Blencowe, B. J., Frey, B. J., Merico, D., Yuen, R. K. C., and Scherer, S. W. 2014. Brain-expressed exons under purifying selection are enriched for *de novo* mutations in autism spectrum disorder. *Nature Genetics* 46: 742–747. doi:10.1038/ng.2980.

U of U Press Release. 2014. U of U scientists create inexpensive way to look inside the brain. *Utah Business*, August 15. Retrieved from http://www.utahbusiness.com/articles/view/u_of_u_scientists_create_inexpensive_way_to_look_i#sthash.7I6YSHkl.dpuf.

Van Nood, E., Vrieze, A., Nieuwdorp, M., Fuentes, S., Zoetnedal, E. G., de Vos, W. M., Visser, G. E., Kuijper, E. J., Bartelsman, J. F. W. M., Tijssen, J. G. P., Speelman, P., Dijkgraaf, M. G. W., and Keller, J. J. 2013. Duodenal infusion of donor feces for recurrent *clostridium difficile*. *The New England Journal of Medicine* 368: 407–415. Retrieved from http://www.nejm.org/doi/full/10.1056/NEJMoa1205037.

Verel, D. 2014a. Genomics—The next set of big data in healthcare? *MedCity News*, August 12. Retrieved from http://medcitynews.com/2014/08/genomics-next-set-big-data-healthcare/#ixzz3ABRaAFXb.

Verel, D. 2014b. Social media pages focused on chronic illnesses are mostly for marketing. *MedCity News*, August 16. Retrieved from http://medcitynews.com/2014/08/study-social-media-pages-healthcare-mostly-marketing/?utm_source=MedCity+News+Subscribers&utm_campaign=afab228b80-RSS_EMAIL_CAMPAIGN&utm_medium=email&utm_term=0_c05cce483a-afab228b80-67008541.

Verizon. 2014. 2014 Verizon data breach report. Verizon. Retrieved from http://www.verizonenterprise.com/DBIR/2014/.

Vestal, C. 2014. Managing diabetes with telemedicine. Pew Charitable Trusts, April 18. Retrieved from http://www.pewstates.org/projects/stateline/headlines/managing-diabetes-with-telemedicine-85899543860.

ViaCyte. 2014. Creating pancreatic beta cell replacement therapy. ViaCyte. Retrieved from http://viacyte.com.

Vutara. 2014. Diffraction technology. Bruker. Retrieved from http://vutara.com/company/company/.

Wagner, D. 2014. 10 robots that could change healthcare. *InformationWeek*, July 22. Retrieved from http://www.informationweek.com/10-more-robots-that-could-change-healthcare/d/d-id/1297442?_mc=RSS%5FIWK%5FEDT&image_number=1.

Wang, S. 2014. New technologies help seniors age in place. *The Wall Street Journal*, June 2. Retrieved from http://online.wsj.com/articles/new-technologies-to-help-seniors-age-in-place-1401749932?KEYWORDS=new+technologies+to+help+seniors+age+in+place.

Ward, L. 2014. Take your heart medicine—And win a prize! *The Wall Street Journal*, June 8. Retrieved from http://online.wsj.com/articles/motivating-heart-patients-to-take-their-medicine-1402062220?KEYWORDS=health+insurance&utm_campaign=KHN%3A+First+Edition&utm_source=hs_email&utm_medium=email&utm_content=13123496&_hsenc=p2ANqtz—cizG2AjbtBw6ovN-v_iUEDJ3gIRz4d4aW9W8LQcuBEQACunByD3ni39UHK2Hf7qQ3Gm0hbnI8ych_GPD0QbZwgGCml_3bJajeRzV4H7_YSUQN1hc&_hsmi=13123496.

Wasserman, E. 2014. Mobile medical app brings laboratory testing to the home. Fierce Medical Devices, June 12. Retrieved from http://www.fiercemedicaldevices.com/story/mobile-medical-app-brings-laboratory-testing-home/2014-06-12?utm_medium=nl&utm_source=internal.

Weinstock, M. 2014. Patient engagement in a mobile world. *H&HN Daily*, July 17. Retrieved from http://www.hhnmag.com/ display/HHN-news-article.dhtml?dcrPath=/templatedata/ HF_Common/NewsArticle/data/HHN/Daily/2014/Jul/071714- weinstock-ochsner-mHealth-patientengagement&utm_ source=daily&utm_medium=email&utm_campaign=HHN.

Weintraub, K. 2014. New stem cells may help in battling multiple sclerosis. *USA Today*, June 5. Retrieved from http://www. usatoday.com/story/news/nation/2014/06/05/stem-cells- multiple-sclerosis/9924469/.

Weise, K. 2014. How big data helped cut emergency room visits by 10 percent. *BloombergBusiness Week Technology*, March 25. Retrieved from http://www.businessweek.com/ articles/2014-03-25/how-big-data-helped-cut-emergency-room- visits-by-10-percent.

Westgate, A. 2014. Most practices face increased HIPAA risks due to security lags. *Diagnostic Imaging*, June 16. Retrieved from http://www.diagnosticimaging.com/blog/most-practices-face- increased-hipaa-risks-due-security-lags#sthash.KpMwLe3S.dpuf.

Wicklund, E. 2013a. Verizon works to bring mHealth to the masses. *mHealth News*, July 3. Retrieved from http://www.mhealthnews. com/news/verizon-works-bring-mhealth-masses?single-page=true.

Wicklund, E. 2013b. Telemedicine comes to the American Frontier. *mHealth News*, August 27. Retrieved from http://www. mhealthnews.com/print/20021.

Wicklund, E. 2014a. Using mHealth to reach Medicaid populations. *mHealth News*, July 9. Retrieved from http://www.mhealthnews. com/news/using-mhealth-reach-medicaid-populations?single- page=true.

Wicklund, E. 2014b. Why providers should care about consumer mHealth devices. *mHealth News*, June 23. Retrieved from http://www.mhealthnews.com/news/why-providers-should- care-about-consumer-mhealth-devices.

Wicklund, E. 2014c. How a home monitoring program slashed hospitalizations and bed days. *mHealth News*, May 27. Retrieved from http://www.mhealthnews.com/news/how- home-monitoring-program-slashed-hospitalizations-and-bed- days?single-page=true.

Wicklund, E. 2014d. mHealth, more important than marriage? *mHealth News*, May 15. Retrieved from http://www.mhealthnews.com/ news/mhealth-more-important-marriage?single-page=true.

Wicklund, E. 2014e. Payers finding value in activity tracking. *mHealth News*, April 10. Retrieved from http://www.mhealthnews.com/news/payers-finding-value-activity-tracking.

Wicklund, E. 2014f. Concierge care gets the telehealth treatment. *mHealth News*, February 26. Retrieved from http://www.mhealthnews.com/news/concierge-care-gets-telehealth-treatment.

Wicklund, E. 2014g. A doc's eye view of mhealth. *mHealth News*, February 13. Retrieved from http://www.mhealthnews.com/news/docs-eye-view-mhealth?single-page=true.

Wicklund, E. 2014h. New alliance seeks upgrade in federal telehealth policy. *mHealth News*, February 12. Retrieved from http://www.mhealthnews.com/news/new-alliance-seeks-upgrade-federal-telehealth-policy?single-page=true.

Wicklund, E. 2014i. Giving caregivers tools to succeed. *mHealth News*, January 29. Retrieved from http://www.mhealthnews.com/news/giving-caregivers-tools-succeed-caremerge-mhealth-mobile?single-page=true.

Wicklund, E. 2014j. Home health monitoring: Tracking what really matters. *mHealth News*, January 7. Retrieved from http://www.mhealthnews.com/news/home-health-monitoring-tracking-what-really-matters.

Wicklund, E. 2014k. New platform offers a yelp for doctors. *mHealth News*, May 14. Retrieved from http://www.mhealthnews.com/news/new-platform-offers-yelp-doctors.

Wicklund, E. 2014l. Telecom giant steps into the virtual visit market. *mHealth News*, June 26. Retrieved from http://www.mhealthnews.com/news/telecom-joins-virtual-visits-market-verizon.

Wicklund, E. 2014m. EyeSpy 20/20: Technology that could save a child's eyesight. Retrieved from http://www.mhealthnews.com/news/eyespy-2020-technology-could-save-childs-eyesight.

Wild, D. 2014. Virtual sepsis unit aids early detection. *Anesthesiology News*, May. Retrieved from http://www.anesthesiologynews.com/ViewArticle.aspx?d=PRN&d_id=21&i=May+2014&i_id=1057&a_id=27391.

Williams, N. T. 2010. Probiotics. *American Society of Health-System Pharmacists*, 6(67) March. pp. 449–458.

Yang, N. H., Dharmar, M., Hojman, N. M., Sadorra, C. K., Sundberg, D., Wold, G. L., Parsapour, K., and Marcin, J. P. 2014. Video-conferencing to reduce stress among hospitalized children. *Pediatrics* 134(1). doi:10.1542/peds.2013-3912.

Yetisen, Ali. 2014. University of Cambridge, United Kingdom. Retrieved from http://www.cam.ac.uk/research/news/pocket-diagnosis.

Yizhar, O., Fenno, L. E., Davidson, T. J., Morgri, M., Deisseroth, K. 2014. Optogenetics in neural systems. *Neuron* 71(1). doi: 10.1016/j.neuron.2011.06.004. Retrieved from http://www.stanford.edu/group/dlab/papers/yizhar%20neuron%202011.pdf.

Zeis, M. 2014. Primary Care Redesign. *HealthLeaders* 17(3)31.

Zimmer, C. 2014. Enlisting a computer to battle cancer, one by one. *The New York Times*, March 27. Retrieved from http://www.nytimes.com/2014/03/27/science/enlisting-a-computer-to-battle-cancers-one-by-one.html?src=me&_r=0.

Index